*"A good name travels from
one end of the earth to another."*

(Midrash Koheles Rabbah 7:1)

Remembering Marvin

The Indelible Footprints Left by Dr. Marvin Hirsch, as Told by his Family and Friends

This book is dedicated in loving memory of Dr. Marvin Hirsch, who graduated with honors in everything he did.

Copyright © 2021 Window View Publications

We would like to acknowledge the individuals and families who gave permission to reprint their materials for inclusion in this book.

ALL RIGHTS RESERVED

No part of this book may be reproduced or transmitted in any form or by any photographic, electronic, or mechanical means, including photocopying or recording, or by the use of information storage and retrieval systems, except for the inclusion of brief quotations in articles and reviews, without prior permission from the publisher.

Window View Publications™
"Scouting Talent—One Book at a Time"™

ISBN: 978-0-9774544-2-6

Table of Contents

Introduction 11
The Family Remembers 19
The Friends Remember 67
Family Tree 145
Timeline 149
Pictures 155
Epilogue 187
Appendix A 195
Appendix B 209

Introduction

"Wise is he who knows what will happen at the end of what is just beginning." (Yerushalmi Sotah 5)

Introduction: Story Time

By Chaim Hirsch

Zaidie, Louie, and Uncle Harry.

Those were the three recurring characters of my father's trademark bedtime stories. Each night, my father would repeatedly chant, "Ding-aling-aling-aling! Stoooooooooooory time!" With those tune-triggering words, my sister Miriam and I would anxiously dive under the covers, ready for the next chapter in his legendary action-packed stories – which were never read from a book. Using his creative gifts and talents, he told us fictitious adventures using the real-life personalities of my Zaidie (my maternal grandfather), Louie (referring to Louie Paltrowitz, Zaidie's friend) and Uncle Harry (Zaidie's brother).

Still unsure as to why these were the three recurring characters, they somehow managed to become staples in our bedtime ritual. My father loved to tell stories, and developed a knack for creating entertaining tales with twists, turns, action, intrigue, slapstick humor, family jokes, and the most important ingredient – cliffhangers – leaving us in suspense until the next night. Most, if not all, of his stories were fictional. In stark contrast, the stories in this book are all real – as told by family and friends. Before diving into the pages ahead, allow me to paint an overall picture of who my father was, and share with you the story – also a true one – of how this book evolved.

My father was diagnosed with cancer when I was twelve, and he spent the last few years of his life on a mission – to find a cure and prolong his life. Each day, he researched the latest medical breakthroughs, from chemotherapy to experimental shark cartilage. He called doctors, consulted top cancer hospitals, and discussed options with friends in the medical field.

Some people get depressed when they get sick. But for my father, it had the opposite affect. He loved life and used his final years searching for a way to continue living. His love for life served as a motivating force for him to conduct research and treat it as his final and most important venture. He appreciated every moment, and what you are reading is a book that celebrates what life meant to him.

In only the fourth verse, the Torah states, "God saw the light was good, and God separated between light and darkness."

If the light was "good" and darkness was not as positive, why did God stop short by just separating them? Why didn't God expel darkness from the equation and just allow the light to shine all day?

Rav Yosef Chaim M'Bagdad explains that the darkness increases our appreciation of the light. God saw that the light was good, but if He were to rid the darkness completely, people would become complacent with light, and not fully appreciate its true greatness. Sometimes, things that seem to be less than perfect may be there to offer a greater appreciation of what you already have.

My father was one of those people who used his disease as a conduit to appreciate life. Some people are intimidated by the curveballs and obstacles of life – but my father used those experiences to fuel his gratitude for the great things that he had. This book is meant to be, among other things, gratitude for having him in our lives.

When I was sitting shiva eleven years ago, a friend pulled me off to the side, away from the multitudes of people. The man first told me how much he loved my father, singing his praises as everyone else had. But then he leaned closer, tightly grabbing my hand like a life raft.

"There's something you need to do," he began. "You need to write the stories and memories of your father in a journal. Put in as much detail as you can. I know it seems petty now, but it will mean something special to you years down the road."

I thanked him for his advice and returned to my seat as the evening continued into the late hours of the night. The visitors continued to pour in and the man's advice quickly slipped to the back of my mind. Weeks went by before I even contemplated his suggestion.

I had such vivid memories of my father's life and what he embraced. Do I really need to write these stories down? If it's crystal clear now, why would it be any different in the future? Could an integral part of my life ever be forgotten?

Just to be safe, I decided to heed the advice of my friend, and keep a journal of the key stories I remembered about my father. I went to the local drugstore, and found a little brown book. It was the perfect size – and price. For only $4.54, I had a journal with empty pages. Now it was my job to fill them.

I never made it my top priority, but anytime I had a few moments, I grabbed the journal and entered a story, dating them as I went along. I laughed. I cried. I thought the whole experience was trivial. It was not conceivable I would ever need to read this journal to revive these experiences – after all, I lived them!

I recently read through the journal that I had handwritten over a decade earlier. While I had recalled most of the stories and memories, the details and specifics were cryptic. It was difficult to recall every emotion I felt and every nuance that happened. And then there were the stories I had completely forgotten. Reading the narrative of such events – in my own handwriting – was incomparable to anything I had ever experienced. It was an experience I have yet to define.

Based on this episode, I contemplated writing a book about my father. Then I advanced the idea. What if I could gather stories and memories from family and friends – people who knew him differently than I did – and create an everlasting treasure for our family? What if I could learn about the person he was in the years before I was born? What if I could piece together a timeline of his life, marking his accomplishments and milestones along the way?

You hold the answer to these questions in your hands.

I am extremely thankful and appreciative to everyone who contributed and shared their thoughts, memories, anecdotes, and stories. Without you, I would only know a small chapter of my father's life. Although I am sure there are many more stories and memories I have yet to learn, your contributions have widened my scope of knowledge about my father's persona and will hold a special place in our family's heritage.

For those who knew my father, I hope you find the pages ahead to be a great tribute to his character. For those who didn't know him, I am honored to present a collection of inspirational stories and fascinating insights about a special individual. It is my hope that when we experience our own challenges and obstacles, the stories in the pages ahead will serve as a motivating force to appreciate life to its fullest – just as my father did through his personal light and darkness.

The Family Remembers

"The crown of the aged are children's children, and the glory of children are their parents." (Mishlei/Proverbs 17:6)

I Remember...

By Corinne Hirsch-Blumenstein

My memories of Marvin are many, and as his wife and the mother of his children, Chaim and Miriam, I want to share some memories that will help shed light on what was so special about Marvin. This is not meant to be a narrative, but rather moments we experienced, which illuminate my memories about him as a husband, father, son, and brother.

In North Miami Beach, the year was 1980 and Chaim was born in December. The bris was held at the Young Israel of Greater Miami, and at that time, Rabbi Zev Leff was the Rabbi of the shul. Several times during the year, Rabbi Leff and the shul conducted full days of classes, usually held on Sundays. It happened that Chaim's bris was held on the same day as one of the full dedicated days to Torah learning. Prior to the bris ceremony, a class was held on bris milah, and it was followed by the actual bris. This was a special moment that Marvin experienced, because the laws of bris milah were being learned, followed by his son's bris with the North Miami Beach and Hollywood communities present.

In 1983, our daughter Miriam was born. The announcement of "It's a girl!" made Marvin so happy and proud. As we were giving birth to Miriam, Marvin's father was also in the hospital. My father-in-law, Irving, had a severe stroke two weeks prior to Miriam's birth. Marvin immediately went to his father's room to tell him that he had a new granddaughter. We spoke into Irving's ear, hoping he would hear and understand our joy, but Marvin was surely emotionally torn at this time, having a new bundle of joy and simultaneously having his dad so critical.

For sure, one of the best memories of Marvin was his love for classical music and his desire to share it with Chaim and Miriam. The classical radio music station in Miami featured a segment on radio every weekday morning called the "Souza Alarm." This "alarm" was played every day to awaken its morning listeners. So, every time the march came on, Marvin would either parade around the room with Chaim and Miriam following along, or each one would take a turn on his shoulders as he did the marching. Till this day, I smile every time I picture this scene.

Marvin was also a truly devoted son. My mother-in-law, Ida, had experienced a tremendous loss and void in her life when my father-in-law died. Marvin looked after his mother with unparalleled care. During the last years of his life, she needed 24/7 supervision. Marvin coordinated her care in all her children's homes so that she would not have to be in a nursing home. This may seem like an ordinary responsibility for a son, but Marvin himself was fighting for his own life at the same time. In spite of dealing with his own cancer treatments, Ida's care was at the forefront of his mind. Because of Marvin, Ida remained at home with us, received the best care, and most of all, was in a loving environment with her grandchildren.

Marvin was diagnosed with colon cancer in February 1993. In 1994, he was being treated for liver cancer. The treatments were on-going until he died in October 1996. Throughout this time, he gained strength from his desire to learn Torah. When he was hospitalized in Houston, a local Rabbi would drop in for a bikur cholim visit. Marvin's greeting to him was, "Rabbi – make my day and give me a Dvar Torah." He would tell Rabbi Davis, "When I walk into shul, my illness is lifted and miraculously it disappears during the time I am here at shul."

I was enlisted as the shul "Mikvah Lady" in 1990. This had me out of the house every night. I could not have done this without Marvin's support. Chaim and Miriam were our main concern, and Marvin was there every night putting them to sleep. It became a very precious time when Marvin announced "story time." Every night, Marvin's imagination was at work telling them stories. It was a series that was continued to the next night. "Story Time" became a special quiet time with stories that the kids can remember from Marvin's imagination.

For many years, Marvin and his brother Ron, ran a college, Heed University (H.E.E.D. was an acronym for Humanistic Education through the External Degree). It is very easy to fall into traps of poor business practices. I was always impressed by the highest standards of ethics in which they conducted business. Nothing was done which could be questioned; their ethics were always based on honesty. This is no small matter in running a business.

Marvin had been recognized by several organizations for his work and tzedakah. During the early years when yeshiva day schools were being formed in the Miami area (about 1974), Marvin was honored for sponsoring full scholarships for a child to go to Yeshiva. When the North Miami Beach mikvah was being organized in 1981, Marvin helped to raise thousands of dollars for this mikvah to be built. He did it because there was a need, not for any recognition.

There were two areas in which Marvin had a desire to accomplish – one was to bring Yiddishkeit to his fellow Jews and another was to live in Eretz Yisroel.

Marvin looked for any opportunity to help other Jews understand Judaism and frumkeit. Our son Chaim has been involved in kiruv (outreach) for many years. As a student at Yeshiva University, Chaim traveled to numerous college campuses throughout the country, conducting educational outreach programs with college students. He continues in this same work in Hollywood, Florida in his speaking and incorporating mussar into each D'var Torah. Chaim's involvement in kiruv is the continuation of what Marvin loved to do. He would have taken such joy in seeing Chaim and his accomplishments.

Miriam has been living in Israel for seven years. It was always a dream of Marvin's to live in Israel. I always tell Miriam that she is living out the dream of her father. When Miriam and Zev's first son was born, the entire event embodied Marvin's spirit. Firstly, the birth and the Brit Milah took place in Israel and secondly, their son was named Mordechai, after Marvin.

The emotions of this day were very comforting to me because through Miriam, Marvin's dream lives on.

Marvin would have taken such pride and nachas in seeing his children live their lives as they are today. Chaim and Samantha with their Rochel Hinda and Miriam and Zev with their Mordechai Yosef, Yisroel Yitzchak, and Aryeh Lev – he would have been the proudest parent and grandfather. Marvin's legacy is his children and all that they and their families embody. May they continue to live their lives in working for K'lal Yisroel so that in their merit it will be an aliyah for Marvin's neshama.

The Two Most Influential People

By Miriam Haller

There are so many things that we learn by living in this world. Some things we learn by experience. Some things we learn in school. Many times we learn from the people around us. But really who should have the most influence on us? A movie star? An athlete? Maybe the guy that packs the groceries has something to teach us. The truth is that the two people that have the most influence in a person's life should be one's parents.

I am very proud to say that I feel lucky enough to be one of the people who has been, and continues to be, positively influenced by my parents. Some of the most important things that I have learned came from my mother and father. Hashem blessed me with 13 years of having my father in my life. Of course my memory does not go back too far, but as far back as I can remember, I have very meaningful memories of my father. The list could be endless with things that I have learned from my father, but I would like to concentrate on a few points.

Strength and bitachon (faith) went together. My father lived and yearned for Torah. When all his strength was gone, he would still go to daven in shul. He would come back rejuvenated. We would ask him where all this energy came from and he would respond that it came from the Aron Kodesh.

Another attribute that my father had was his ability to listen to people's problems no matter how big or how small. Jew or non-Jew, long or short story, he had advice for everyone. He gave every person a feeling of love, warmth, and kindness.

His love for classical music gave our house a very peaceful atmosphere. I hope to continue this path that my father paved and learn from his beautiful way of life.

I would also like to express how much I have learned from my mother. There is no way my brother and I would have made it if it wasn't for my mother. Never once did she show us how hard it was for her to carry on with normal life. Always with a big smile on her face, my mother would give the shirt off her back to anyone. I have learned so much from her strength and ability to function when life gets hard. There is no prayer in the world stronger then a parent's prayer for their child.

People may look at my situation as sad and unfortunate, but I know this is what Hashem wanted for our family. And I know that my father is praying for us all the time in Heaven so close to Hashem.

Not only did my parents build their home, but they helped to build my home, too. I will never be able to fully thank my father and mother for what they have given me. One way I hope to thank them is by continuing in their line of chesed and give to my children as much as they gave to me and the people around them.

Two Paths

[Editor's Note: Reprinted from an essay written by Miriam Hirsch-Haller when she was in seminary]

This Rosh Chodesh Chesvan is 5 years since my father passed away. In life, we do not have many choices. "Man plans and God laughs." Five years ago, I had a choice. The choice of a dead-end path destination – going nowhere, or the path of Derech Hashem (the way of God). No choices are easy, but this one was a little harder than "paper or plastic." It is so much easier to give up and go down. Then, I decided what path to take.

But before deciding, I thought, "What would my father want me to do with my life?" My father passed away before he could accomplish many things. That is why I chose Derech Hashem. I am not only living my life, fulfilling my dreams, accomplishing my goals, but they are also my father's. That day that I was lost and didn't know the way, I was scared. However, I knew that I had two fathers looking down at me showing me the way.

Golden Memories

By Gladys Heiman

[Editor's Note: The following is a letter written from Cousin Gladys to Marvin's sister, Fradelle]

Dear Fradelle,

Having grown-up with Marvin, nobody knows him better than you and Ronnie. However, I do know that he had a heart of gold for everyone and loved people. He was most generous with all that was within him and this enabled him to keep his school going. Marvin had a winning smile which I'll always remember. Needless to state here, I loved Marvin and to this day, I still miss him, along with his mom, my dear Aunt Ida.

Love you too, Fradelle,

Cousin Gladys

The Little Brown Book

By Chaim Hirsch

The Angel of Death & the Power of Tehillim

Shortly after my Bar Mitzvah in 1994, my father traveled to M.D. Anderson in Houston, Texas, one of the top cancer hospitals in the country. The plan was to go there with his brother, Ronnie, surgically remove a large cancerous tumor in the liver, and come home before Pesach.

The surgery seemed successful as the doctors were confident they had removed the cancer. My father and Ronnie checked out of the hospital and into the rehabilitation center across the street, planning to return home only a few days later. My father went to the bathroom and unexpectedly collapsed. Ronnie rushed him back to the hospital, where they ran many tests to determine the cause. As fate would have it, an infection had found its way into his body during the surgery and was independent of the cancer. The infection strengthened, and my father soon landed in the intensive care unit. The week before Pesach, my mother traveled to Houston, as the doctors were less than optimistic that he would live through the experience.

My father later recalled an incredible episode that occurred at some point during this six week time period. He related how he had felt extremely cold, closed his eyes, and saw snow, ice, and a hazy sky. Then, coming out from the distance, my father remembers seeing the Malach Hamaves – the angel of death – coming out of the shadows, waving a sword! My father instantly screamed to Ronnie to start reciting Tehillim immediately. As Ronnie started to recite Tehillim, my father recounts that the ice started to melt to water, the snow started to recede, the sky turned blue, and the angel of death slowly started moving backward, waving his sword in anger, as if to say, "I will be back for you."

Ronnie was there the whole time, who confirmed the story as my father had experienced it. Interestingly enough, when my father came back from Houston and relayed the story, he asked that I not talk about it with people. But he articulated that this incident proved to him the power of Tehillim. My father was convinced that it was the recitation of Tehillim that kept him alive through that incident.

As an interesting side note, when people would come to visit him, they would customarily ask, "What can we do for you? How can we help?" My father often replied very simply, "Say a little Tehillim for me every night – that's what you can do."

Junior, the Delivery Man

During the summer of 1996, the last summer my father was alive, he had trouble doing what many of us take advantage of – breathing. To assist him, oxygen tanks were delivered to the house weekly. One day when I was home, a delivery man arrived with the weekly oxygen tank supply. The muscular gentleman with a goatee – nicknamed Junior – came into the house, dragging the oxygen tank behind him.

As he went back to his truck to get additional tanks, my father whispered to me, "I'm counseling Junior." With a shocked look, I said, "That guy? The delivery man? You're counseling him?"

My father continued to explain that Junior was divorced and encountering a difficult time dealing with his ex-wife and the custody of their kids. I was a little skeptical of all this, considering Junior was just the delivery man! Granted, my father was a guidance counselor many years ago in a New York high school and loved to help people. But Junior – a mere acquaintance he knew on a weekly basis?

Several months later, after my father had passed away, Junior returned to collect the remaining empty oxygen tanks. As he pulled them out of the house, Junior said to me, "You know, your father made a big difference in my life. He really gave me good advice and inspiration. I'm going to miss him."

My father wasn't kidding when he said he counseled Junior. Such a story was just one of the many indicators of how he took interest in and cared for people – even if it was a delivery man he barely knew.

A Different Type of Medicine

Although my father was not a formal Gabbai at the Young Israel of Hollywood-Ft. Lauderdale, he went to morning minyan every day. During the early years of the shul, there were only about fifteen to twenty people on a daily basis, and because of the limited resources and small nature of the shul, he took out the Torah almost every Monday and Thursday from the ark.

During that last summer of his life, I accompanied my father to shul on Monday morning. He would say to me – time and time again – "I feel very sick physically, but as soon as I open the ark and take out the Torah, I start to feel better. It's almost as if the kedusha (holiness) of the Torah is going into my body and healing me!"

Strangely enough, as soon as we would leave shul and get into his 1982 blue Toyota Corolla, my father complained of feeling sicker as we drove home, seemingly losing more energy from just moments earlier.

This didn't just happen once. For many weeks afterward, my father continued to relate how he would gain more energy and have a lapse in pain when he opened the ark. At first I thought it was a fluke, but as I heard and witnessed it on multiple occasions, I realized he really meant it.

The Desire to Learn

My father always had a passion for learning Torah. Whenever I had a day off from school or was on vacation, he would motivate me to learn with him. Over the course of several years, we finished the Mishnayos of Rosh Hashanah, Yoma, and Succah, among other random works along the way. I expected, as he got sicker with time, that his physical desire to learn would diminish, and it would be with less intensity. But I was wrong. In fact, it was just the opposite.

Towards the end of his life, when he was sleeping almost two-thirds of the day, he would wake up, and tell me to bring over a Chumash or Mishnah to learn. Even if it was small in time, it was very big in energy and enthusiasm. And incredibly enough, after we would learn each time, he would say, "I think I feel a little better."

His desire to learn never diminished or vanished. Instead, it was actually fueled by his illness, and while most people would have lost interest, he wanted to use every remaining moment to the utmost of its potential.

Five Minutes Later

During one summer, I was home from school in the early 1990's, and would accompany my father to shul. He noticed there were several teenagers coming to minyan, and wondered what they were doing with the rest of their free time. He spoke to a few of them, and realized that some were working, others were doing book reports, but not many of them designated any time to learn Torah. So my father proposed to the teenagers that they learn with him just five to ten minutes after the morning minyan. I was surprised that several of them agreed to it.

While my father was not a Rabbi or advanced scholar, he enjoyed learning. Every day, after davening, my father would pull out a Chumash or Mishna and learn with all the teenagers for five to ten minutes, just as he had promised. I always looked at it as a "nice thing" he did, but otherwise did not attribute much merit to it. Several years later, I discovered how wrong I was.

Nearly half a decade later, after my father died, one of the teenagers from that group told me what that learning did for him. He explained that it inspired him to appreciate learning on a whole new level. That person continued to learn in a yeshiva for many more years. I was stunned and amazed at how a short five to ten minutes of learning made such a difference in someone's life.

Coincidence or Timely Message?

In the summer of 1998, at the age of seventeen, almost two years after my father had passed, I was entrenched in an elaborate project. For three consecutive years earlier, I had been involved with Mussar Haskel – a weekly publication that the students of Yeshiva Toras Chaim wrote and disseminated, based on the discourses delivered by the Rabbeim. The students worked with the Rabbeim and several other faculty members to ensure it was accurate and well written.

The one-page publication was distributed to some of the major shuls in South Florida. Once we had three years worth of material, we compiled the weekly issues of Mussar Haskel into a book, called *Courage to Change*. One of the primary goals in compiling this book was to mail it to over 1,500 people on the Yeshiva's mailing list and use it as a fundraiser right before Rosh Hashanah.

In a beautiful gesture, the Brauser and Milrad families co-sponsored the book in memory of my father. It took about eight months to complete, including editing, formatting, proofreading, cover design, printer coordination, and fundraising to sponsor the cost of the project.

There was a day in mid-July 1998 where things looked bleak. I had gotten very far with the process, but there were some key elements that had imploded and it appeared – for a short while – that the entire project would be on hold. I had been working on this since January 1998, and suddenly it had come to a screeching halt. It was frustrating and disappointing, considering how much work had gone into it thus far. And then the package came.

Within the same week of dreary events, my mother received an envelope from Rabbi Glatt, a prominent Jewish educator in South Florida (and also my fifth grade Rebbe). The cover letter said the following (paraphrasing): "Your dear husband, Marvin, had compiled a pamphlet many years back which he sent to the yeshiva to use. This pamphlet was given to Rabbi Chait (one of the Roshei Yeshiva), and he passed it along to me. I have used it in my teachings, but thought you would like to have it."

Enclosed with Rabbi Glatt's package was a pamphlet – a bunch of papers folded together that had my father's handwriting on it. They were basic question-and-answers about Judaism, such as the reason for wearing a Yalmulke, washing one's hands before eating bread, etc. My father hoped that the yeshiva boys could put together a Q&A pamphlet of this nature and disseminate it among the community, as positive publicity and possibly a fundraiser for the yeshiva.

The timing of this package's arrival was incredible. Here I was, putting together a project that encompassed all the same features my father had hoped for – students and Rabbeim working together to disseminate a work used as positive publicity and a fundraiser for the yeshiva! He envisioned this many years earlier and was delivered to me the week I needed it most! And even more fascinating is how appropriate it was that *Courage to Change* was being dedicated in his memory. The combination of all this was enough to give me the last bit of inspiration and motivation I needed to complete the project.

[NOTE: Equally of notable interest was the timing of when my father had written these questions. I was astonished when I saw the date on it – not because my father had done this, but because of *when* he had done this. In the last five years of his life, my father went to shul, possibly attended a brief shiur, and then came home to research the best methods to battle his cancer. Where did he find time to write an entire pamphlet of Q&A's on Judaism? Nobody paid him to do it (at least not in this world), and he wasn't getting any recognition for it (our family didn't know about this until two years after he had died!). But that's the type of person my father was – one with limitless love for Torah, yeshivas, and mitzvos.]

Family Ties

My father died with everyone around him: his wife, two children, two siblings, my future in-laws, and a Rosh Yeshiva and my high school principal (they were there the night earlier). My father had a loving group surrounding him when he left this world, which I always perceived to be a tremendous blessing. What did my father do to have this merit?

In Parshas Noach, the very first verse says, "These are the offspring of Noach, and Noach was a Tzadik – a righteous person."

Many commentaries wonder what the connection is between these two thoughts. What is the link between Noach's offspring and the Torah informing us of his righteous devotion?

Rav Moshe Feinstein answers that the correlation is based on the limitless and boundless love a person has for his children. People are intrinsically born with a love for their offspring. They will do anything and everything for them. There are no boundaries or limits. And that's exactly how Noach performed the Mitzvos in living a Torah lifestyle: he did it with limitless love and devotion. That's why the verse places these two thoughts together – to teach us that just as Noach loved his children with sincere loyalty and limitless love, so too, he lived a Torah lifestyle in the same manner.

While it is not our place to speculate, perhaps one of the reasons my father merited to have his entire family around him when he died was because of his loyal commitment to a Torah lifestyle. He epitomized someone who knew no boundaries when performing mitzvahs and doing good deeds. He had limitless love for Torah, yeshivas, and mitzvos. Maybe – just maybe – that's why he had the merit for his entire family around him when he died.

Growing Up with Uncle Marvin

By Chaya Hirsch

I am 7-years old, and I love going to see Uncle Marvin and Aunt Corinne. I don't have any brothers or sisters, but that doesn't matter; I always get to play with my cousins in Hollywood! Uncle Marvin's house is beige and red. When I visit, Uncle Marvin has classical music playing. It comes from the clock-radio in his room on the dresser. He has a garden in the backyard with juicy red tomatoes and my favorite: crisp, green peppers! I love it when it is my turn for Uncle Marvin to push me on the tire swing. While I am swinging, he sings: "She flies through the air with the greatest of ease..." Aunt Corinne *always* has something good to eat waiting in the kitchen. Sometimes she makes spaghetti and meat balls for me. Her chocolate chip cookies are out of this world.

Sometimes we all go to Grandma's house. Grandma has two dogs, Max and Tinker. She also has a swimming pool, so we all get to go swimming at Grandma's house. Uncle Marvin's favorite stroke is the side stroke. We have races in the pool, jump into the water, or just make waves with the floats. Uncle Marvin will also put us on his shoulders. Sometimes we'll play on the swing set. Miri and I eat ice cream on the tall, yellow chairs at the kitchen window on the porch. Then we have to wait before we go back into the pool. Uncle Marvin takes us back and forth from Grandma's house in his little red car. In the summer it is so hot that we stick to the vinyl seats.

I am 9-years old, and I know that Uncle Marvin, Aunt Corinne, Chaim and Miri live at 3881 North 49th Avenue. I know because Uncle Marvin told me he chose the number 49 for his lottery ticket. He told me it was lucky for two reasons: one is because his house is on 49th Avenue and the other is because my daddy is 49 years old. My parents and I go to Uncle Marvin's house on Sundays. We also go for special occasions like Mother's Day, Father's Day, or Thanksgiving. I don't like eating turkey, but Aunt Corinne bakes the best pumpkin pie! We also go for birthdays. I remember one of Chaim's birthday parties in the backyard with all of his friends. We also call Chaim "Big Chaim" because he's the oldest cousin and the older Chaim. At Big Chaim's birthday party I thought it was funny when he couldn't blow out the birthday candles on his cake – *THEY WERE TRICK CANDLES!* Sometimes Big Chaim plays his violin for us.

I am 11-years old. Uncle Marvin calls me a *Baala Busta,* because I love to cook soup. I don't cook just any soup; Uncle Marvin and Aunt Corinne bring me Cream of Mushroom soup from Elmira when they visit Bubby and Zaidy. When Uncle Marvin calls my house, he tries to teach me how to count to ten in Yiddish. I usually make it to drei, three. Sometimes, I go to Uncle Marvin's house for Shabbos. That means getting up early in the morning for the first minyan. After davening we stay for the kiddush. Some Shabbos afternoons we all walk to Aunt Fradelle's house to visit. One Shabbos Big Chaim, Miri, Little Chaim and I had a home-made charif eating contest-we all took as much of the spicy charif as we could on as little challah as possible. All our mouths were burning!

Now I smile at the sight of a tire swing – too bad I am now too big to swing on one. I enjoy the occasional piece of classical music when I hear one. A worn out fisherman's hat is all it takes to make me nostalgic. I always try learning how to count in other languages. These are just a few of my small, everyday reminders that I am fortunate to have of my childhood with Uncle Marvin.

Through the Years

By Dr. Ron Hirsch

My Big Brother

Marvin was quite a Big Brother. He was a role model for me and Fradelle. Much of what I learned was because of him. By the time of my tonsillectomy (five years old) I knew the names of all the bones in my arms, legs, shoulders, etc. He taught me everything that he knew! History, psychology, political science, economics, and geography, among other subjects.

I went with him to museums, the botanical gardens, and the Bronx and Prospect Park zoos. We fed peanuts to the squirrels. We took trolley cars until they were replaced by busses.

We were always together and I wanted to be like him and do as he did. We both went to City College. We both had appendectomies. We both had pilonidal cystectomies. We both taught at Zichron Moshe. We toured Israel together. We both worked in Brentwood. We both were involved with Heed University from its inception until his passing. We lived next door to each other in North Miami Beach. We shared the same moving truck and moved from Newland Gardens the same day. His funeral was Monday, October 14, 1996 – also my birthday.

Brooklyn

I remember living in Brooklyn until 1950, when we moved to the Bronx. Marvin attended the Yeshiva of Brooklyn, where he was strongly affected by and influenced by its founder, Rabbi Mandell. He had his Bar Mitzvah in a Brooklyn shul.

His appendix was removed while we lived in Brooklyn. Hospital rules prevented me from visiting, but I observed his room from outside the building.

He attended Boys High School for the first two years of high school. He wanted to travel from the Bronx to Brooklyn to finish high school, but traveling was too time-consuming. He often took me to the Prospect Park Zoo, where we fed peanuts to the squirrels. We traveled by trolley until they were replaced by busses. He taught me about baseball, which of course meant the Brooklyn Dodgers and their hated opponents, the New York Giants and New York Yankees.

We lived in Brooklyn when Fradelle was born. When mom and Fradelle came home from Beth Israel Hospital, we had already moved to the Bronx. Uncle Natie drove them home from the hospital.

The Bronx

We moved to Mace Avenue in the Bronx in April 1950. Marvin earned his high school diploma from Christopher Columbus. During college vacations, he traveled by bus to Asbury Park or Lakewood, New Jersey to work as a busboy or waiter.

After graduation from City College in 1956, Marvin bought the family's first car. It was a black, two-door, 1950 Oldsmobile. He took us everywhere! We went home, shopping in Queens and Spring Valley. On Sundays, he took us to visit our paternal grandmother and uncle Louie, who lived on Hoe Ave in the Bronx. We went yearly to Mattawan, New Jersey, to the cemetery where our maternal grandparents were buried. Although I was under age, he taught me to drive on the cemetery grounds. Afterwards, we visited Tanta Sophie and cousins Louie and Shaynie in Keyport, New Jersey. In 1960, he bought a two-tone 1954 Chrysler.

His first teaching experience after college was at Yeshiva Zichron Moshe on Morris Avenue in the Bronx. His next teaching experience was at junior high school Number 139 in Manhattan. He also attended and earned his Masters in Guidance and Counseling from the Graduate School of

Education of Yeshiva University in 1960. He earned a Professional Certificate from Queens College in 1965. He became a guidance counselor at South Jr. high school in Brentwood, New York in 1960.

He bought a new 1963 Chevrolet Impala so he could travel safely to work. He was one of the first to cross the Throgs Neck Bridge and was present at its dedication. In August 1962, he helped the family purchase our first home on Radcliff Avenue in the Bronx.

In the summer of 1964, the family and Queenie, the family dog, traveled by car to Los Angeles to visit Tanta Annie and cousins Itzynu, Elaine, and Karl. Marvin did most of the driving. We left Tuesday morning and arrived in Los Angeles the following Sunday at 2 P.M. I bought my first cowboy hat at a rest stop in Oklahoma. We stopped overnight near St. Louis, Missouri and spent Shabbos in Albuquerque, New Mexico at the foot of the Rocky Mountains. We toured the Grand Canyon and the Painted Desert. This trip was awesome.

Exciting Rides

I had a final exam just after a Jewish holiday. I would be late – very late – if I took a bus. Marvin drove me – what a ride! I was only a "little" late.

Another time, our family (without Queenie) were going to Marvin's afternoon graduation from Yeshiva University. Traffic was sluggish. Suddenly a huge fire truck was directly behind us, air horns and sirens blaring. After what seemed like an eternity, we moved out of its path. We managed, with God's help, to get to where we were going, relatively on time.

We drove safely, keeping to the speed of traffic and not exceeding the speed limits by too much. We paid careful attention to traffic reports and weather conditions. We took highways that were clear of slow-downs due to construction, accidents or congestion.

Once on the Queens side of the Throgs Neck Bridge, we took the Cross Island Parkway to the Southern State (Belt) Parkway, Northern State (Grand Central) Parkway or the Long Island Expressway to Brentwood. We sometimes took north/south roads between the above routes if conditions warranted.

Brentwood

He was a guidance counselor from 1960 to 1973. One of those years, he was employed as Director of Research. His round trip was almost 100 miles per day. In 1965, I joined him as an elementary school teacher in the same school district. We traveled together and for several years, we had a car pool with two other teachers.

We each took a two-year leave of absence from 1973 to 1975, when we retired from Brentwood and continued our commitment to Heed University in Hollywood, Florida.

Hollywood

Marvin came to Florida for first the time during winter vacation in December of 1964. He drove with his friend Jerry and took mom and Fradelle along. Mom stayed in Miami Beach and he and Jerry "found" Hollywood Beach.

In 1969, we "rediscovered" Hollywood Beach in search of an office for the future Heed University. Our first offices and classes were held during the summer of 1970 on Hollywood Beach at the Carlsbad Motel. In subsequent years, our offices were at North Young Circle, Monroe at 20th, Johnson Street & A1A, and the Home Tower at Young Circle and Harrison Street.

Classes were held during winter and spring vacations, and July and August at the last three locations. Marvin and I lived in downtown Hollywood. We eventually had offices in Beverly Hills, Los Angeles, St. Croix, the Virgin Islands and Milwaukee, Wisconsin. We met many wonderful, fascinating people through Heed University. Many are considered among our best friends.

Our family purchased a home in Hollywood Hills, Florida, and relocated there in August of 1974. Marvin and Corinne were married in February of 1980. Chaim was born in December of 1980 and Miriam in August of 1983. Marvin was proud of his family. Our expanded families celebrated birthdays, anniversaries, and holidays together.

Texas Medical Center; M.D. Anderson Cancer Center

Marvin's health problem began in the 1970's and 1980's with several surgical procedures. In February of 1993, cancer was found and a regimen of chemotherapy followed.

By September of 1993, it had metastasized to his liver. Again, after considering various options, I accompanied Marvin to the M.D. Anderson Cancer Center at the Texas Medical Center in Houston, Texas. We arrived there February 28, 1994.

Following several days of testing and consulting, his colon was re-sectioned on Friday, March 4, mom's birthday. The surgery was long but successful. We were advised, however, that the cancer would likely return. Erev Shabbos, we were visited by Rabbi Eliezer Lazaroff of Chabad of the Texas Medical Center. Marvin inquired as to the health of "The Rebbe!" As was typical Marvin, he was more concerned with another person than about himself.

Our stay in Houston was supposed to last two weeks; however, numerous complications were to occur that extended his stay. Two weeks post surgery, Marvin was released to our room across the street at the Rotary House. He collapsed in my arms on the way to the bathroom and was rushed to the emergency room.

He credited me with saving his life on a number of occasions. He claimed to have several near death experiences from which I rescued him. One night he complained of feeling very cold and saw the "Angel of Death" approaching. He asked me to recite prayers and Tehillim/Psalms with fervor.

On another occasion, he again saw the "Angel of Death" approaching and Marvin used his boxing skills to fend him away. Another time, he refused to have x-rays taken because he didn't want to be like the "others."

He spent nine weeks at M.D. Anderson. Six of those weeks were in isolation in the Intensive Care Unit due to a serious systemic infection. He was placed on a ventilator. He had two additional surgical procedures on March 21st, his birthday, and March 31st.

Corinne joined us for a period of time. The staff at Anderson was superb. The Houston Jewish community could not have been more supportive. The Lazaroff's, the Munks, and the Kornfeld's merit special mention for their concern and support. Drs. Wally Fingerer and Morty Freiman were especially supportive and consulted regularly, on a course of action with Dr. Mark Roh, Chief of Liver Surgery at Anderson. Dr. Roh was marvelous in his surgical, medical skills, and his concern for Marvin and me. We returned home to Hollywood on May 4, 1994!

Young Israel of Hollywood-Ft. Lauderdale Dinner

On March 5, 1995, Marvin and Corinne were honored at the annual Young Israel of Hollywood-Ft. Lauderdale shul dinner. The event was to pay tribute to Marvin for his participation and dedication to the shul from its early days and Corinne as the "Mikvah Lady" for so many years.

At first, Marvin and Corinne were reluctant to accept the honor, but after much encouragement, they graciously consented. It was a beautiful event filled with singing, dancing, and meaningful speeches. This was our turn to be proud of Marvin and Corinne.

Unfortunately, earlier that day, Corinne's mother, Hennie, became ill and went to the hospital. She passed away exactly one year later.

Final Shabbos at Hollywood Medical Center

"Could you spend Shabbos with me?" Marvin asked. "Of course." I responded. "If I could spend six weeks with you in Houston, Texas, I can spend Shabbos with you in Hollywood, Florida."

He mostly slept. Especially since he controlled the amount of medication he received by pushing a button. Lynette, his aide, spent most of Shabbos with us. The family gathered after Shabbos.

A doctor, who was on call, asked me why Marvin was being kept alive??!! I explained his belief in God and his desire to live and enjoy his family. I related the ordeal at M.D. Anderson, and had we answered that question negatively, he would have missed several pretty good years.

Insight and Reflections

Marvin loved life. He loved Torah. He loved knowledge. He loved people. He loved his wife, Corinne, and children, Chaim and Miriam. He loved his parents, grandparents, brother, and sister. He loved his aunts, uncles, and cousins.

He loved to share in the joy and success of others. He was kind, compassionate, and generous. He was always optimistic. He always saw the good in people. He was always happy and wanted to make the family happy. His greatest nachas was to make others happy, particularly his family. He was a truly remarkable man.

His legacy is Chaim, Miriam, and his grandchildren, as well as the lives of everyone with whom he had contact. Be it at Yeshiva Zichron Moshe, JHS 139, Brentwood Junior High School, Heed University, Young Israel of Greater Miami, and Young Israel of Hollywood-Ft. Lauderdale. This was my mentor, my big brother!

The Shirt off His Back

By Samantha Hirsch

It is usually quite common for a young girl to find her parents slightly embarrassing. Most girls grow up with little memory of those years, either because they have been totally forgotten or just permanently blocked. One way or another, most venture into adulthood with the knowledge that like their parents before them, someday they will be privileged to slightly embarrass their own children. It is a definite right of passage that most look forward to. The following story is one such embarrassing moment as it relates to Marvin Hirsch.

I could write an entire book, or at least a whole chapter on how Marvin and Corinne were instrumental in bringing my family to frumkeit. The extremely abridged version would be that Chaim said a bracha at my third birthday party, prompting my parents to move me into a more religious day school. We became frum, grew up, Chaim and I got married and now we live happily ever after. But before all of that could happen, my father had to embarrass me on one sunny Shabbos afternoon.

I must have been around fourteen years old as my father accompanied me to the Hirsch home so that I could visit with Miriam. It was our usual Shabbos ritual, and on this particular Shabbos, my father thought that he would join me and visit with Marvin.

We arrived at the door and Miriam came to greet us. Marvin was sitting on the couch without a shirt on and upon seeing us, he began to rise. My father asked him not get up, as clearly he was not feeling well. Marvin looked down at his exposed belly and told my father that he was embarrassed and would be more comfortable if he put a shirt on.

Not wanting Marvin to inconvenience himself or to be embarrassed, he promptly did something that is forever etched into my mind as possibly one of the top ten most embarrassing moments with my father. With the whole Hirsch family in the room (and possibly some other close friends, but I have most assuredly blocked that part out) my father looked down at Marvin's belly and swiftly tore off his own shirt. There he was, in all his glory with his belly hanging out, as he plopped himself onto the couch next to a smiling Marvin.

The two shirtless men began talking as if it was nothing out of the ordinary while I gaped in horror. (Keep in mind that at fourteen, anything even slightly strange is embarrassing when done by a parent). They sat there like that, talking and laughing all afternoon. Other community members came to visit Marvin and each time someone entered, there they sat, two shirtless men, as if it was a common occurrence. Marvin welcomed in each guest with a big smile and bare belly.

I don't remember how the day ended, nor do I remember how long it took for me to get over my supreme mortification. What I do remember is that when I was fourteen, my father was uncomfortable with the thought of frumkeit. It was uncommon for him to willingly attend shul, and equally uncommon for him to befriend people who were as steeped in frumkeit as Marvin was. Yet, he transcended those feelings and developed a deep and wonderful friendship with a man who knew no judgment.

What was once a briefly embarrassing moment in time, taught me the power of acceptance and love. Marvin accepted my father with his whole heart; a deeply powerful gift that I know has never been taken for granted. We are all better people for having known him, and especially for having been loved by him.

It was the mere fact that Marvin never judged others that led my entire family to embrace a more enriching lifestyle. A lifestyle that eventually led to my wonderful marriage and subsequently to our beautiful daughter. It saddens me that I never got the chance to truly know such a warm and loving man, and even more so, that our daughter won't have that chance.

I know however, that through her father, as well as the wonderful memories inscribed in this book, she will grow to know exactly where she came from. Her life will be imbued with the lessons and love that her father received from his father and maybe, just maybe, a little dose of embarrassment.

Our Cousin, Marvin

By Selma Kotler and Frances Grossman

[Editor's Note: The following two letters were sent to Chaim by Marvin's cousins, Selma Kotler and Frances Grossman]

Dear Chaim,

My earliest memory of Marvin goes back to around 1937 and 1938. Grandma Ida moved into the first city housing in Williamsburg. Marvin was quite young and his mom used to bundle him up with scarves and sweaters. Your grandfather was working for the Academy of Medicine in Manhattan and he had access to the signs MD's used, and he had one for Marvin – "Dr. Marvin Hirsch" – hanging on the door, like all Jewish moms and dads, they had ambitions for their kids.

My sister's sentiments rings true about your dad. During one of my father's stays in Florida, he had some heart contractions and was hospitalized. Marvin visited him daily, and looked over him. My father talked highly of Marvin and appreciated it.

One other mitzvah Marvin performed: My father insisted that when he passed on, no Rabbi be present to officiate. When he did pass away, I wanted to obey his wishes and came up with a wonderful substitute – Marvin. He came up and officiated at the gravesite and returned to Florida on the same day. Chaim, I could not forget it.

Selma

Dear Chaim,

I remember Marvin in a very loving and caring manner. He was a person who loved and cared for family and friends. My father loved visiting Marvin in Florida. My father would always speak very highly of Marvin. My father would tell us about Heed University and how he liked hanging out at the school with Marvin and Ronnie. He would kibbitz with everybody. Marvin always treated my father with respect and great love. My father loved you and always spoke your praises. He would tell Marvin what a great kid you were and how well you played the violin.

Marvin was a wonderful person and good husband and father. I am enclosing a picture which shows my father as a graduate of Heed University – it reflects my father's sense of humor, and Marvin's good nature.

Cousin Frances

The Tztitzis that Never Got Hushed

By Barry and Carole Lynn

A Special Pair of Tzitzis

It was my wife, Carole, who led our young family back to traditional Judaism. I'll admit that even though I am a staunch traditionalist, I was not quite so enthusiastic about getting involved in prayer and Jewish rituals. Most were foreign to me. In shul, I felt awkward and out of place.

We knew the Hirsch's from Beth Shalom. Samantha and Chaim were in the same pre-K class and were good friends. So it was only natural that when we moved into the neighborhood, the Hirsch's were among the first families to welcome us into their home. Marvin and Corinne were not just "welcoming," they actually made me feel like an "insider" instead of an "outsider."

Marvin had such a talent for making you feel like an old friend. But it wasn't really a talent, because "talent" implies skill, and it was really just part of Marvin's personality. Marvin's friendship made it much easier for me to continue attending shul and move forward with my Yiddishkeit.

One day, for no apparent reason at all, Marvin gave me a gift of my first pair of tzitzis. Had anyone else given this to me, I would have felt that they were trying to force more Yiddishkeit upon me. But from Marvin, it was a very special gift. Marvin's special acceptance of me encouraged my growth of Yiddishkeit. I always cherished Marvin's friendship. But what I did not realize until after he was gone, is that he helped create my life and the life of my family. Without Marvin's wonderful influence, I would not have two frum daughters today. And I would not have such an incredibly wonderful son... Chaim Hirsch... whom I dearly love and at whose wedding I wore my special pair of tzitzis.

Hush Puppies

As a board member for American Friends of B'nai Zion Hospital in Haifa, I was entitled to receive 4 free tickets to the annual gala "black tie" dinner event. One year, I received an additional perk – a special invitation to a private VIP Reception for visiting dignitary, Benjamin Netanyahu. Carole and I were very excited about the opportunity to meet Netanyahu. We decided to invite our dear friends, the Hirsch's, to join us.

Unfortunately, Carole underestimated the time necessary to get prepared for this lavish event. As the clock was ticking, my level of anxiety was building. I didn't want to miss a moment with Netanyahu. After only 10 minutes or so, Carole was ready. The sun was going down as we drove to the Hirsch's. I tooted the horn and Corinne and Marvin immediately appeared, both decked out in their very best formal dinner attire – Marvin in a tuxedo and Corinne in a very lovely evening gown.

At the hotel, we left the car with the valet and headed inside. As we got off the elevator, right in front of the VIP Reception room for Benjamin Netanyahu, Marvin looked down at his feet and noticed that his shoes didn't exactly match his tuxedo. It seemed that he always left his comfy, but somewhat ragged Hush Puppies by the front door. By habit, on the way out of the house, he slipped on his Hush Puppies instead of his patent leather formal shoes.

Most people would probably have been very embarrassed to be seen looking like this at such an auspicious event. But Marvin had an amazing sense of humor. He laughed, and then moved forward to meet Netanyahu with his head high and dignity completely in tact.

I Never Left Hungry

Marvin was a special friend. He was not judgmental, and if he was, he probably saw only the best in people. I really enjoyed being with him, even when he was ill. Towards the end, he was mostly confined to bed. Whenever I could, I would stop by the house to visit. He was always happy to see me. I was always ready and willing to massage (fancy word for rubbing) his aching back. While I was rubbing, he was talking – but never about himself. Instead, conversation always focused on other people and his concern for their well being. That was probably Marvin's most incredible attribute: he always cared more for others and went out of his way, WAY OUT OF HIS WAY, to help those he loved.

As a fledgling Ba'al Teshuva, the rituals of Shabbos did not come easily to me. But a meal at the Hirsch's was something I looked forward to. Needless to say, Corinne's renowned reputation as one of Hollywood's finest chefs made any meal tempting. But Marvin was the one who really fed the soul.

Having very little background and being thrust into an Orthodox community, I found myself intimidated and embarrassed by all I did not know. In Marvin's mind, I believe I represented an opportunity for him to help someone grow in Torah. He was so incredibly sensitive to my feelings of inadequacy that I learned from him without even realizing that I was learning Torah. At the time, I thought it was Chaim whom he was teaching. Now that I think about it, I realize how clever Marvin was. He knew Chaim knew the answers to all his Torah questions, and I would therefore learn from Chaim. And how right he was! Nothing was more enjoyable than learning Torah from Marvin and Chaim.

Memories of Uncle Marvin

By Chaim Milrad

Marvin Hirsch was someone I am proud to say was my uncle. From the little I can remember, he was very caring, and epitomized what many consider to be the main principle of the Torah, "V'ahavta l'rei'acha kamocha – Love Your Neighbor as Yourself." He used to give me coins and stamps which sparked my interest in collecting. Many people just gave presents, but my uncle went a step further. He would explain many details behind the coin, stamp, or other item in a way that made you even more interested and excited in receiving the gift. I remember clearly how he used to be a fan of Thomas Jefferson and would discuss some of his historic background when discussing the two-dollar-bill and nickel.

Another memory I recall is how he used to play games with me. This ranged from chess, which required much of his time (he may have even taught me how to play; I don't remember), to physical playing, which took much of his energy. We played chess many times and he always made it more exciting with ongoing commentary and constantly letting me win. He would also get on the floor and play army men, "Cowboys and Indians" with me, telling stories and making it much more fun.

There were also a number of times where we would play "circus," where I would lay down flat on the bed, and he would lean his chest on my outstretched legs, relying on my legs to support his body weight. Pretending to be the announcer for a circus, he would say "Ladies and Gentlemen, Children of All Ages..." He then proceeded to build the anticipation by announcing, "First, I will be upheld by two feet," and I would keep both feet extended on his chest. Then he would say, "Now, the right foot!" and I would release my left foot, leaving only the right foot on his chest to uphold his weight. He followed this with, "Now, the left foot!" and I would go through the same motions. He would then say, "And now something which has never been attempted and done before: no feet!" I would then remove both my feet from his chest, leaving nothing to support his weight, and he would slowly fall on me and we'd have a great laugh.

My uncle was truly an unbelievable individual who made every person, even little me, feel special and important. He didn't just do something, he did it with passion and with his full effort. I learned a tremendous amount from him, especially how it's so important to treat every person with respect on his level and to always give your full effort in all you do.

My Wonderful Brother Marvin, My Hero

By Fradelle Milrad

Few in years, many in deeds
Always smiling and loved by all
Touched our lives with kindness and compassion
May his memory continue to inspire us always.

Although Marvin and I were 15 years apart, we could not have been any closer. Marvin was always there for me. From a young age, I remember Marvin taking me so many places, like the park, the zoo, Lincoln Center for concerts and ballets, amusement parks, and family trips.

When I was six, I got a piano. Marvin was instrumental in helping to get the piano. He always enjoyed listening to me play, especially when I got more proficient and played classical music.

In October 1957, I remember Marvin driving my parents and me to the hospital to have my tonsils removed. I remember the black car, carrying a small suitcase, and a doll. They told me after my tonsils were removed I could have all the ice cream I wanted. Wow, that would be great. Not so the first few days, but after that it was wonderful.

I remember all of us driving to Marvin's graduation from Yeshiva University. We were all so proud of Marvin. It was an outdoor commencement and there was a huge crowd. Since I could hardly see, I had to stand up on the bleachers. It was a beautiful, sunny day. I will never forget the joy on my parents' faces.

I would often accompany Marvin to a gas station where a dog named Tuffy lived. Tuffy had puppies and I had to have one of the puppies. I had the pick of the litter and chose an adorable female I named Queenie, a miniature German shepherd, who was so smart and beautiful. Queenie went all over with us, including our trip to California. Eventually, Queenie had her own litter of puppies. Marvin and I were with her when each puppy was born. Marvin and I shared this very special time together.

In July 1964, Marvin drove our family cross-country to California to visit relatives. We stopped at so many landmarks and beautiful parts of the country. Marvin always appreciated nature's beauty.

When I was 14, I worked one summer in Marvin's office in Brentwood. There I learned to type and file. I drove back and forth each day with Marvin. It was my first summer job and I loved it. Marvin's secretary, Miriam Friedman, taught me so many things and I grew very fond of her. We are still in touch.

I was so excited and thrilled when I got my acceptance letter to Hunter College in the Bronx in April 1968. I remember calling Marvin in Brentwood with the wonderful news. He was so happy for me and shared in my excitement. I knew I wanted to go into education, just like Marvin and Ronnie. And that is exactly what I did. I completed my B.A. and M.S. from Hunter College, and went on to teach elementary and special education. I also substitute taught in Brentwood for a while before getting a permanent position with the New York City Public Schools.

One of the saddest things I remember is when I had to call Marvin one Friday morning in May 1970. I told him Queenie passed away. It was a very turbulent time in our country with the Vietnam War protests and Kent State shootings. After Shabbos Marvin buried Queenie in our backyard. It was a very sad time.

One summer in 1972, when I was visiting Florida, I became ill. I had an infection and had an adverse reaction to medication. I had trouble breathing. Marvin rushed me to Memorial Hospital where I got treatment. Marvin was always there for me.

In the summer of 1973, Marvin got sick and Ronnie and I drove him to North Shore Hospital in Miami where his surgeon Dr. Gerber practiced. Marvin was running a high temperature and was lying down in the back seat shivering and very cold. Since he had a high temperature, the surgery was postponed. Ronnie and I stayed with Marvin over Shabbos to be close to him.

In August 1974, Marvin, my parents, and I took the auto train and moved from the Bronx to Hollywood, Florida. We were all looking forward to moving into our new home. Ronnie was waiting for us at the house when we arrived.

I got a teaching job in Ft. Lauderdale and then taught in Hollywood for one year. In July 1976, I decided to join Marvin and Ronnie at Heed University. It was the best decision I made. I loved working together with my family. My dad worked in the library and sometimes my mom would come up and help also. Many times we would have lunch together.

There were so many happy occasions with our weddings and similar events. Ronnie married Anna in November 1977. Marvin married Corinne in February 1980, and I married Jeff in August 1980.

Then along came Chaim Hirsch (December 1980), Chaya Hirsch (April 1982), Chaim Milrad (July 1983), and Miriam Hirsch (August 1983). There were birthdays and anniversaries to celebrate together.

Marvin was my Chaim's sondeck at his bris in July 1983, Marvin held him on his lap the whole time. It was very emotional for Marvin. From that time on, Marvin spent a lot of time with his children and my Chaim. He showed my Chaim so much love and told him wonderful stories and played games. Chaim loved it and always loved being around Marvin. Marvin was so good with children and had so much patience. Marvin was such a good storyteller.

It was so wonderful when we all got together and had so much fun. We all enjoyed the pool at Grandma's house. The kids learned how to swim there. It was so nice sharing these happy times.

I wish these happy times could have lasted forever. Unfortunately, my mom passed away in August 1996 and then

Marvin in October 1996. It was my faith and strong belief in Hashem that got me through this dark period of my life. My dad had already passed away in August 1983. He got pleasure in seeing Chaim Hirsch and Chaya Hirsch. My dad suffered a stroke two weeks after my Chaim was born and passed away when he was one month old. He never knew Miriam, who was born just 4 days after he had his stroke. I wish he could have lived to see more naches from his grandchildren.

The last simcha for my mom and Marvin was my Chaim's Bar Mitzvah in July 1996. My mom passed away exactly 8 days after his Bar Mitzvah. Marvin was already very sick and weak, but his spirit was strong and he survived another 3 months.

We were all with Marvin when he passed away on Sunday, October 13th at 5:55 PM. He was surrounded by the love of his family. He would never have to suffer anymore and would be in a beautiful place with my parents.

I was very lucky to have Marvin for my brother. He was a gift from Hashem and I was so thankful that Marvin was in my life. I could never have chosen a more wonderful brother.

Life was good having such a terrific brother like Marvin. Marvin was so nurturing, supportive, loving, a wonderful role model, and always there for me. I looked up to him and always sought his opinion and approval. He taught me to be positive and optimistic. Marvin's motto was, "I'm happy when you're happy!"

Marvin rescued many animals, like birds, rabbits, and dogs. He loved animals, especially dogs. Once he rescued a German Shepherd, who we named Princess. Another time he rescued a mutt and found a good home for her. I followed Marvin's lead and rescued many dogs. I shared his love for dogs.

Marvin was also a humble man who cared about people and always tried to help and offer his advice. Marvin had so many wonderful qualities and virtues and was looked up to and respected by everyone.

Marvin was a unique person. He was a born leader; intelligent, energetic, charismatic, creative, with a dynamic personality. He was such an inspiring and innovative educator who touched so many lives.

Marvin took great pride in studying and learning Torah. He received much nachas seeing his children learning and growing in Torah. Marvin was keenly interested and supported Torah learning and gave a lot of Tzedaka.

Marvin had everything except length in years. I value and will always cherish my memories. He stood for everything good and was so dedicated and devoted to his family and friends. I was so proud to say Marvin was my brother.

Marvin left such a legacy – his two children, Chaim and Miriam – whom he loved and adored so much. May they be a merit to his neshama.

I miss Marvin so much and can only hope and pray that he is in a better place until Moshiach comes. May Moshiach come now. Amen.

A Devoted and Kind Man

By Jeff Milrad

I remember meeting Marvin on my first trip to Florida. He was very likeable, pleasant, and friendly. As I got to know him more, I liked him even more. He was a mensch, very devoted to his family.

Marvin was a heavy smoker. I remember how hard he tried to quit. He was so determined and had such perseverance. I remember he would keep a toothpick or plastic straw in his mouth to keep from smoking. He was always kind to me and I will always remember that.

Thicker Than Blood

By Dorothy Sall and Family

At our cousin Joy's Bat Mitzvah in Florida during the mid 1990's, I was approached by Corinne and Marvin Hirsch. Marvin was fighting for his life and discovered an experimental treatment out of UC Irvine that required blood and specifically not from a blood relative. I was honored to be asked to be a donor of blood and was thrilled at the possibility of extending my brother-in-law's life. I traveled to UC Irvine and went through a screening test to see if I was a suitable donor, and sure enough, I was. The day arrived and Marvin, his brother Ronnie, and I all met at UC Irvine. My Dad, a retired doctor and professor, also drove up from Mission Viejo to be there with me and watch the procedure.

We optimistically gathered and were hopeful that this procedure would be effective. As I started to give blood, the machine shut down and my blood did not flow. Repeated attempts were made to take my blood (even with the bed inverted to help the flow), but the alarm bells sounded loudly. It was agreed that I was unable to give blood, as my veins kept collapsing around the needle. I started to sob and felt like such a failure. It was Marvin who comforted me. He explained that I had done a mitzvah just by my willing to be a donor. I will never forget the impact that Marvin's soothing words had on me that day. He was the one fighting for his life, yet his kindness in the face of my despair will be forever etched in my memory of him.

All in the Family

By Rabbi Vam and Gloria Schwartz

When we were living in New York, Gloria's sister came to visit the Hirsch family in Florida. Fradelle picked her up from the airport, and she proceeded to have a wonderful time with the entire Hirsch family. When she came back, she marveled at how Irving and Ida Hirsch had a "true Florida home, which included a pool!"

A few years later, we would move to Florida. We moved on a Tuesday in February 1980, and the following Sunday was Marvin and Corinne's wedding. We attended the beautiful wedding and were thrilled to rekindle our relationship with the family.

Marvin was a special person who was outgoing and friendly. We remember visiting his creation, Heed University, and seeing how proud Irving was of his son. Marvin assigned his father, Irving, to take care of the library. Irving took pride in setting it up and maintaining it. It was clear that Marvin performed an amazing chesed by giving his father a job as the librarian. It gave Irving fulfillment and a sense of purpose. We admired Marvin for making his father a part of the Heed University team.

We also saw how Marvin and Ronnie worked together with such incredible love. There was an amazing and beautiful shalom between the parents, children, and siblings. We also remember the family's intense love for dogs.

When Marvin decided to move to Hollywood in the early 1980's, he truly had foresight as to what the community would become. Marvin was instrumental in laying the foundation and groundwork for the Young Israel, which started as a small house. He helped build it from the floor up, and today it is a thriving and growing community.

In the early 1980's, we started a "Tehillim Club," where we encouraged people to say designated portions of Tehillim during a specific time period, and through the collective efforts of the group, the entire book of Tehillim would be recited. Marvin enthusiastically participated by reciting his assigned portion of Tehillim and also inspired others to join as well.

Marvin was a special person who came from a special family, all of whom exhibited an incredible love for Torah, mitzvos, and family.

Leading the Way

By Allen and Aviva Zweben

Allen and I remember Marvin as being so welcoming and reaching out to us. He immediately called us, "Cousin Vivi" and "Cousin Allen" as well as calling my late beloved parents, "Aunt Chanee" and "Uncle Hym." We were all one family.

I was living and working in Milwaukee and knew one of Marvin's old friends, Rabbi Tzvi Tsur who was the community Chaplin in Milwaukee. He recalled Marvin's leadership in South Florida to build Young Israel when Tzvi lived and worked in South Florida. We will always remember Marvin as a welcoming and warm person who displayed great leadership in his community.

The Friends Remember

"Four things are better old than new: wine, fish, oil, and – more than the others – a friend" (Talmud Ta'anis 23a)

Smiley Face

By Rabbi Seymour Atlas

I met Marvin in November 1990 when I moved into Hollywood. When I entered the shul, the very first person to greet me was Marvin. He welcomed me with his trademark jolly smile, asking if there was anything he could do to make my transition smoother.

Our friendship developed rapidly. Every time I got an Aliyah at shul, Marvin would come over and jokingly remark, "I knew they would get the right guy," and then escort me back to my seat.

I remember visiting Marvin in the hospital during the earlier days of his illness, and I clearly remember him saying, "Rabbi, don't worry, I'm going to get out of here. The doctors don't know everything." And sure enough, he did get stronger and healthier and lived for several more years after that.

Even when he was ill, Marvin laughed, to the extent that an outsider would never have even known Marvin was in pain. I would walk with Marvin in the hospital, and he would tell me, "You have no idea how much I appreciate you coming to see me here."

Several years later, when he was bedridden and nearing the end of his life, I went to visit him. I clearly remember how he retained his beautiful smile. Marvin could still talk, and towards the end, Marvin said, "Whatever Hashem has in store me, I will be his candidate and I'll do what he wants me to do." Shortly thereafter, he passed away. The funeral was a beautiful tribute to Marvin.

Marvin was a wonderful person. He wasn't just a good friend – he was also an inspiration to the shul and community. He always made people feel like they were part of a big family. I never saw Marvin without a smile. He was one of the friendliest people I ever met, and I think about him often.

His seat was very close to mine in shul, and his son, Chaim, now sits there. I can still see his image in that chair, with his vibrant, glowing smile that never disappeared – even after all these years.

Open House

By Julie and Moshe Averbuch

Our memories of Marvin are his amazing warm smile and ability to make you feel special. I think this is what attracted my father to Marvin. Whenever my dad visited us from Israel and went to the Young Israel, Marvin was amongst the first to always welcome him.

As always, when Jews get together, they immediately play the "who do you know" game. As it turned out, we shared very dear friends who were both special education teachers of severely handicapped children. Sharing these friends in common brought my dad and Marvin's relationship to a higher level. Their conversations were often about Israeli politics and the love for Israel that they both shared.

As for myself, during our initial years in the Hollywood community, I organized Shabbos afternoon groups for the children of the Young Israel. Even though Chaim was seldom at other people's homes, that didn't stop Marvin and Corinne from offering their home when it was their turn. I walked the boys over and never left. It was not because the Hirsch home was not safe or that my boys pulled on me begging me not to leave; quite the opposite. The boys took off to play and learn parsha. Marvin, with his warm hospitality, asked me to sit, offered me some of Corinne's best, and our conversations took off. *I will always cherish those special Shabbos afternoons.*

He has left behind a beautiful legacy.

Graduating with Honors

By Jack, Ann, and Michael Bailen

Marvin was not only compassionate to anyone who needed someone to talk to, but he was also a son that all parents would like to have. He spoke to or saw his parents every day. His brother and sister looked to him for advice, as Marvin was a good listener with broad shoulders. When Marvin founded Heed University, his parents and family were involved and worked for the school. He knew he could trust and depend on them.

I never heard Marvin utter a negative word about anyone. He had only good things to say. He could not see a bad side to any person he came in contact with.

Marvin loved his family and friends. Whenever Marvin saw me or my family, he always would invite us for a Shabbos dinner, even if he already had a house full of guests. There was always room for two, three, or four more. He was a truly devote and righteous man.

What big shoes for children to walk in. Chaim and Miriam, I believe, will fill those shoes because their genes come from a great and honorable man.

Marvin and the Beautiful Dried-Up Esrog

By Rueven and Elka (Robert and Ellen) Balgley

When Marvin went for one of his early cancer surgeries in the early 1990's, he received an interesting piece of advice from a Rabbi in the family. The Rabbi told him to tape Hadassim leaves (from the Lulav & Esrog used on the Succos holiday) onto his chest. The concept was that something that was used for a mitzvah would bring good mazel during the surgery. Although Marvin had never heard of this ritual before, he was happy to try anything that had a spiritual component. He went to the hospital, and with the doctors inquisitively looking at him, they ultimately agreed that they would place the Hadassim leaves in his pocket during surgery. Thank God, the surgery was successful.

Fast forward several years later, after Marvin had passed away, Ellen was pregnant with our fourth child. During the pregnancy, some have a custom for the pregnant woman to bite the pittum (stem) of an Esrog, as it is a merit for her not to be in pain during labor. Ellen performed this custom during the holiday of Succos. At that time, we didn't know how an Esrog would soon make a life-changing impact on our lives.

Several months afterward, Corinne saw that Ellen was pregnant and offered assistance. She volunteered to baby-sit at any time – day or night. On the night that Ellen went into labor, we took Corinne up on her offer. We called her late at night, and she rushed over to our house to watch our three boys. When she arrived at our house, she handed Ellen an Esrog. We both looked at Corinne in confusion, knowing that Succos had already passed several months earlier, and said, "Why are you handing us an Esrog?"

Corinne then explained that it was important to take something with us to the hospital that was used to perform a mitzvah, as it would bring good mazel. She quickly recounted the story of the Hadassim leaves and how it helped Marvin recover during one of his early surgeries. She explained that Marvin always felt from that point forward that when you use something for a mitzvah, it retains an intrinsic value that brings mazel.

During labor, Ellen held onto the Esrog all through the contractions. Thank God, the birth went well, and we had a new baby girl.

Then came the decision of what to name our new daughter. In Hebrew, when combining the first letter of our other three children's names – Shimshon, Meir, and Chaim – it spells the word "Samyeach – Happy." We therefore decided it would only be appropriate to have our new baby's name begin with the Hebrew letter "Hay." This would ensure consistency in that the first letter from each of the four names of our children would spell "Simcha" – which also means "happiness."

Still undecided which exact name to use, the community Rabbi explained the urgency of naming the baby that Shabbos, as it would be the first time the Torah was being read after the baby was born. Ellen and I picked about six to eight preferred names that began with the letter "Hay," wrote the names on small pieces of paper, and placed them into two cups – one for me and one for Ellen. We both picked out a name from our respective cups, and as fate would have it, we both chose the exact same name – Hadara, which means "beautiful." We knew it was meant to be that our daughter would be named Hadara.

It wasn't until years later that we realized a striking connection between our daughter's name and the spiritual component that went into her birth. We found it astonishing that our daughter's name, Hadara, is mentioned in the Torah when it says (Vayikra 23:40) "Pri Etz Hadar – Fruit of a beautiful tree" – and is explained by Rashi to mean an Esrog! The name Hadara – which was chosen by chance – is interpreted as an Esrog, and was given to us by Corinne when

Ellen went into labor! It was only because of Marvin's strong feeling about the intrinsic value of mitzvos that Corinne thought to bring us an Esrog.

To this day, people comment to us how beautiful Hadara is, and when we explain her name means "beauty," it resonates the true magnificence of the story.

The story continues even through today. Just recently, in May 2008, Robert's sister was having her first child in over 13 years. Ellen informed her of the Esrog, and how it seemed to have a spiritual significance. Robert's sister held onto the Esrog during her labor, and thank God, gave birth to a beautiful baby boy.

At the hospital, the doctor and nurses were all asking about the Esrog's significance and why she brought it. Robert's sister proceeded to explain all the aforementioned events. The doctor – a non-affiliated Jew – found this to be fascinating and kept asking questions about Judaism. One thing lead to another, and within the next few days, the doctor was learning how to put on Tefillin and recite the Shema!

It is astonishing that this all began from Marvin's firm belief that there is intrinsic holiness in the performance of mitzvos. Marvin was an incredible person with whom we shared a special relationship. It's amazing that even with him gone, he continues to impact the people around him – and even some he never met.

An Eternally Happy Face

By Dr. Billy and Batzi Berman

One of our first memories of Marvin was at his wedding in February 1980. Needless to say, he was exceedingly happy - and that happiness remained for as long as we knew him. We remember him always greeting us and our children with great interest and enthusiasm.

We were amused because he took pride in being mistaken for the grandfather of his children. Others might have been uncomfortable or irritated with such comments – but with his good sense of humor and big smile, he only saw it in a way that imbued pleasure and delight.

Corinne and Marvin were honored by the Young Israel on March 5, 1995, at a time when Marvin was already ill. Unfortunately, it was the same day that someone else in the community died, causing a paradoxical mix of emotions between tragedy and celebration. To their credit, Marvin and Corinne were able to create a dignified balance between the desire to continue the dinner and the heavy-hearted feeling in the room that evening.

We visited Marvin many times during his illness and despite the pain and discomfort, he always had a smile and a positive thought. Whether it was his wedding, raising children, consoling members of the community in tough times, or fighting through his illness, Marvin was always there with an upbeat attitude and cheerful smile.

A Good Ear

By Rabbi David Botton

As a teenager growing up in Hollywood, I spent a significant amount of time around Marvin in the shul and at shiurim in the community and his home. I was fortunate to be able to help him prepare Seudat Shelishit (the third meal) almost every Shabbat from when I was fourteen years old until he no longer was doing it. That time was special for me as I would discuss with him many of my personal thoughts.

He always had clear insights into life and living. He had a big impact on me and my growth in serving Hashem. He was always positive and always had a smile. When speaking with Marvin I always felt he attributed value to all I said and treated it with the utmost of importance, regardless of what it was about. From Marvin I learned the incredible importance of a good ear to help others.

The Power of Amen

By Joel Brauser

Marvin was sick for quite a while, and over the course of his illness, I went to visit him several times. Towards the end of his life, I remember his willpower and how he struggled, using an oxygen tank when he was short of breath. When I went to visit him with my daughters, it brought Marvin so much joy that we had come. It was a mutual feeling, as my girls also liked playing with Pepe, the family dog.

During the last week of Marvin's life, I went to visit him at Hollywood Medical Center, where he was being treated. It was at night, and as I was talking with him, Marvin made what appeared to be a bizarre request. He asked me to daven Ma'ariv out loud, so that he could answer Amen to each of the Brachos that I said. Marvin was so weak at that point that it was hard for him to have a full conversation, let alone daven. Marvin's deep commitment to Yiddishkeit became amazingly clear. For someone who had little time left, his overpowering desire was to respond Amen to the brachos that I recited.

I remember rubbing and massaging Marvin's back, which he also loved and very much appreciated. Marvin was a sweet and tender man who I constantly miss and will never forget.

The Massaging Words of Torah

By Michael Chesal

My most meaningful memories of Marvin are probably from my visits with him in the hospital in the last year or so of his life. On several occasions, it was just me and him, one on one. He would routinely ask me to "talk Torah" with him. When I could muster something up, it was as if you could see the words of Torah giving him small injections of life. He would always light up with a smile. (Luckily I knew to prepare something in advance.)

He would then usually ask me to massage his back from the pain that unfortunately even the words of Torah were not strong enough to mask. At first, it was kind of uncomfortable. But then I realized that if he was willing to ask me to massage his back, it was because he felt close enough to me to ask. And that feeling of closeness meant more to me than anything. I began to view those back massages as a big honor.

If the accomplishments of one's offspring can be a measure of one's success in life - and I'm pretty sure that's a fair yardstick - then Marvin surely deserves the highest of accolades. His children are shining examples of what it means to live a true Torah life, with boundless dedication to the good of the community. I am sure Marvin is looking down from his 50-yard line seat in Shamayim beaming with Yiddishe nachas at his children's accomplishments. What more could a parent ask for?

May his memory be a blessing.

Glowing Reviews

By Howard Chusid

Marvin was a real sweet man who had a GREAT BIG SMILE! I remember how proud Marvin was of his children. In particular, I recall the times we were sitting at Kiddush after the Shabbos early morning minyan. I was at one end of the table, and Marvin was at the other end. He was talking with one of the people next to him. Then Chaim got up to give a short Dvar Torah. Marvin started glowing. He intently listened to each word that Chaim said, and Marvin clearly had a large inner smile. He always smiled outwardly, but there was a special inner smile that consumed him. Towards the end of Chaim's speech, he continued smiling, but then his inner glow shined and everyone could see it on his face. Anytime Chaim got up to speak, it was that inner shinning that couldn't be missed.

There were times we all knew Marvin was in pain. The hurt showed throughout, but just by mentioning the names Chaim or Miriam, it was enough to cause a noticeable change in Marvin's demeanor. He was always so proud of both Chaim and Miriam. The pain was always there, but it was subjugated to a different plane. I guess Marvin and Corinne did pretty well.

Magical Memories

By Sharon Clements

When Marvin was ill, he frequently needed shots and required a nurse to administer them. The last 6 months or so of Marvin's special life, I was pregnant with our twins, and I was on partial bed rest. That meant not working and resting a lot during the day, but not staying off my feet 100%. I developed a special relationship with Marvin on the phone, telling each other little quips and just checking in with one another frequently during the day. I was also very fortunate, for living around the corner from the Hirsch's was an easy and convenient way for me to help by giving Marvin his shots. He would tell me stories that would put a smile on my face.

Marvin loved to see our children, (Miriam was 7 and David was 5 at the time) so they accompanied me whenever possible to the Hirsch's home. David remembers Marvin to this day for his uncanny humor and kid-friendly magic tricks. Our son specifically recalls when Marvin "magically" pulled a quarter out of his ear. It was just one of the many things he would do to entertain and bond with the children in our community. He also gave the kids some special cards about Eretz Yisrael. One has been hanging proudly on our refrigerator for all these years as a memory of a special person. Now it is going back to Chaim to have another keepsake. When Marvin passed away, we lost much more than a neighbor around the block – we lost a special friend and community member.

Engraving a Lasting Impression

By Drs. Alvin and Tammy Cohen

In honor of our 25th wedding anniversary, we donated a metal breastplate to be placed over one of the Torah's at the shul. Shortly thereafter, someone mentioned that while it was a beautiful idea to have the breastplate dedicated, it would greatly enhance it if it were engraved with the dates of our marriage.

I casually asked Marvin if he knew of any resources to do the engraving work. Marvin didn't know of any places off hand, but took the initiative to find an engraver. He located a unique business on Johnson Street – a baseball trophy retailer – who also did engraving! Next thing I knew, the engraving was complete on the beautiful breastplate!

All I did was ask Marvin if he knew of any places that could do this work. I certainly didn't ask him to spend time and effort researching and locating an engraver, but he went out of his way to help – even when I didn't ask for it.

Marvin and his son, Chaim, sat next to me in shul since the Young Israel of Hollywood-Ft. Lauderdale was first built. It was an honor to know him, and while we all miss him dearly, his memory remains alive every time we take out that Torah.

Enthusiasm, Ardor, and Zeal

By Dr. Stuart Courtney

The Torah portion of Tsav, in the book of Vayikra (Leviticus), speaks of the responsibilities of the priests, the Kohenim. For the individual Kohen to be effective, he was required not only to perform his duties, but to do them with enthusiasm, ardor, and zeal.

The latter three qualities precisely describe how Marvin Hirsch (z"l) went about his business, particularly when there was a mitzvah to be performed. Whether it was attending to his aging parents (where he was an incredible and constant role model in performing "kibud av v'aim"), or running an errand for the shul, such as setting up a kiddush, or fixing the eruv, or any request the Rabbi might suddenly thrust upon him, Marvin Hirsch scurried to do it with enthusiasm, ardor, fervor, zeal, and alacrity. There was a constant smile and a ready laugh that made him fun to be around; and, to his credit, the smile and positive behavior remained even when severe illness robbed him of his physical health.

When the President of the Young Israel of Hollywood, one of the speakers at his funeral in 1996, remarked, "Marvin Hirsch will be missed by all those who knew and loved him," everyone in attendance silently and solemnly nodded yes. Dr. Hirsch is still deeply missed to this very day.

Remembering Marvin Hirsch

By Dr. Jeffrey and Judy Dach

Back in 1981, the shul was only 50 families, so we were a small community and pretty close knit.

Since the old days, a lot of people in the shul have passed away. Joe Rubenfeld, Marty Feigenbaum, Irving Kahan are a few names of people I remember. Some people are easy to remember, some aren't. It's funny how memories of these days of the shul and these pioneer shul members are clear for some and faint for others.

Marvin was one of those personalities you always remember with vivid clarity; he had this sort of easy saunter, ear-to-ear grin with an easy laugh. Marvin was the kind of guy who would see the humor in any situation, and make a brutally honest comment, and then laugh about it with his hoarse raspy laugh. At the same time, he was a very sensitive individual, and would never hurt anyone's feelings.

Marvin and Corinne (the "Mikvah Lady") had us over to their house for Shabbat and Marvin told us about his correspondence school, and we met their daughter and a little red haired kid, who was their son.

Marvin was devoted to his family and he used to wait in the carpool area to pick up his kids after school. If my daughter Karina came out first ahead of his kids, she would run into his arms, he would pick her up giggling, and they had a great old time.

One year, Marvin and Corinne were the honorees for the shul dinner. Over the years we have been to a lot of shul dinners, and honestly I can't remember the speeches of any of the honorees with the exception of Marvin's. That's the kind of guy he was – memorable.

He was at the podium the night of the dinner in his tuxedo, and commented on how the dinner selection committee had a difficult time because many of the candidates for honoree had declined to accept. So, Marvin said, "The next time they call on you and ask you to be the shul dinner honoree, go ahead and accept it, because it's really not all that bad."

That's the kind of dry humor he had. "It's really not all that bad," he said, and then he grinned and laughed. And he had a great time at the dinner. By then, we all knew that Marvin was seriously ill, but he was still good, and we were glad to be able to celebrate with him.

So if you ask me, do I remember Marvin? Yes, Marvin was the kind of guy everyone remembers. That's the kind of guy he was.

How to Win Friends and Influence People

By Stuart Dalkoff

Marvin and Corinne were designated by the Young Israel Congregation of Hollywood-Fort Lauderdale as our host-welcoming family when we moved to Hollywood in June of 1993.

The Hirsch home became for us like a 2nd home – and we looked forward to their warm open door policy, encouraging one to come over and visit on Shabbos. Marvin and Corinne warmly welcomed our visit and enjoyed discussing personal, community, political, and Jewish current events until it was time to go to mincha or until the end of Shabbos.

Marvin seems to have invented the expression "making lemonade out of lemons." His warmth glowed and one could not help but try to catch on to some of it…his outlook on life was happy, positive, and he loved people. He spoke ill of no one, and he was the personification of how to win friends and influence people.

My mother always remembers Marvin for his devotion to his mother, Ida, in her final years. She speaks of how he tended to her needs when her strength and physical abilities limited her capacity to care for herself. Marvin did so with the greatest of love and devotion any child can pay to a parent. This was at a time, let us remember, that he himself was very ill.

Marvin was a selfless man and his happiness came from giving, not taking.

In our son's room, we have a framed poster taken at the first Florida Marlin's game of the first baseball to be used at that game, delivered by a US Postal Service truck. Marvin knew we were at the game and that we loved the game of baseball. In addition, we still have two tumblers (Texaco-Florida Marlins 1994) presented as a gift from Marvin.

We think of him often...and we *know* we were privileged to be his friends, albeit for a few short years. He taught us lessons about love of life, love of Torah, and what is important and meaningful.

A Timely Message

[Editor's Note: This was a handwritten letter sent to Marvin less than two months before he died. The letter was dated Saturday night, Motzei Shabbos, August 24, 1996]

Dear Marvin,

A few weeks ago, I began a note to you. I never completed it.

Perhaps you are not fully aware of the inspiration and role model you are to people. When you come into a room, people want to say hello, to shake your hand. You always have a smile – a good word – a good thought for people.

Many people are petty and self-centered – we worry about silly, stupid things. We have our priorities all mixed up. It always seemed to me that you knew what your priorities were – what is important in family, community, and religious life.

To me, you are someone who has captured the essence of what it means to be a Torah observant Jew – to combine Mitzvos of L'Makom (to Hashem) with Mitzvos L'chavero (to your friend and fellow human being).

This is what shines, what stands out most to me when I think about you – the important lesson of loving people, loving Hashem, and having a smile on your face. I know the smile on your face has mirrored the smile of your soul.

I really mean it when I say you are a special example to us ordinary people who seem to be stuck in the mundane levels of trivia that most people are stuck with.

You always to me have been an example of the finest and kindest that can be brought out in people. Many people respect, admire, and love you. It goes without saying that we have been praying for you.

Your inspiration, kind, gentle, and uplifting manner are very important to us, and we are proud and grateful to be able to call you a friend.

Stuart Dalkoff

A Prayer a Day Keeps the Pain Away

By Rabbi Edward Davis

I wish to share 3 vignettes about Marvin. The first two deal with his years of illness. When I would visit him, he would insist that I had to tell him a Dvar Torah before I left. No matter what condition he was in, lying in bed or sitting at the table, alert or drugged, he would be floating on a spiritual high when I spoke of Torah. I realized after several of these sessions that his euphoria was not due to my Torah knowledge. Not at all. It was the psychological high that he was able to reach through hearing the words of Torah, no matter if they were brilliant or mediocre. It was not the substance that counted; it was the spirit. To date, I have never been able to reach Marvin's level of spirituality. For me, all of Torah depends upon substance and intellectual ability. Marvin captured something far deeper and meaningful. I always left his presence feeling uplifted.

The second vignette was also during his years of fighting his cancer. There were many mornings that he was able to manage to get himself to Shul for the morning services, even though he was in quite a bit of pain. He put on his Tallit and Tephilin and sat and stood during the 30-40 minute recitation of prayers. At times I saw him saying the words. Other times he was too fatigued and was satisfied with listening and following along. When we were finished, everyone was hurriedly moving to exit to start the busy day. Marvin lingered and was in no rush to leave. I asked him if he needed any assistance. He declined my offer and explained his slow pace. He found that when he was in Shul like that, in Tallit and Tephilin, he was pain-free. As soon as he returned to his car, the pain would return. So all he wanted to do was to remain in Shul and soak in the ambience that provided him with such relief from his struggle with the cancer.

The third vignette was back in 1983. I was about to go to Russia to teach Torah for two weeks to Refuseniks in the Jewish underground in Moscow and Leningrad. I was told that I would need a new passport that was not marked with the stamp of Israel. I also needed to apply for a tourist visa that would not indicate that I was a Rabbi. When Marvin heard about this, he immediately resolved my latter issue. Marvin was the head of Heed University and had an ID made that showed that I was a full professor of history at the university. It was a true act of kindness on his part that helped me. In return, I came frequently to teach some Torah to Marvin, his brother, and several others who stopped by.

These stories are a small demonstration of how Marvin felt about Torah and the type of kindness that was commonplace in his daily routine.

The Legacy Continues

By Baruch and Zohara Epstein

We moved from Brooklyn to Pembroke Pines in November 1987 and then to Hollywood in 1998. We always wanted to be in an Orthodox Shul, so from day one we went to the Young Israel of Hollywood.

Our first encounter with Professor Hirsch was at the Synagogue. He was extremely friendly and received us absolutely magnificently. He was always a welcoming person who asked how we are and how we were getting acclimatized to South Florida. We developed a very good, heart-to-heart friendship. We started to have extremely interesting discussions in matters of Torah or our professions.

Every Shabbat, I saw Professor Hirsch, and toting behind him was a lovely son and daughter. I always saw them engaging in Torah discussions or school matters. On the day that his son became a Bar Mitzvah, and after hearing his speech, I remember vividly Rabbi Davis telling him and the Kehila – "Chaim you are thirteen going on twenty-three." I looked into the eyes of Marvin as well as his wife Corinne and saw a moment of Nachat. All of us, including my wife Zohara, had tears in our eyes. The same evening, I will never forget the Melaveh Malka at Young Israel with all the warm feelings and Divrei Torah given. What an occasion.

Later on, when Marvin had to go for radiation to Jackson Memorial, we had the honor of taking him several times. During these trips, we always had engaging and interesting discussions, even though he suffered greatly.

He passed away about two weeks after our younger son's murder, yet Zohara and myself made sure to participate in the funeral for such a good friend.

During the years, we have now developed a lasting friendship with Chaim and his wonderful wife, as well as the new little princess. If at all possible, I try not to miss Chaim's Shabbat speeches at Aish.

There is a Chumash at Aish which was donated in memory of Professor Dr. Marvin Hirsch. My wife Zohara – before the start of the Shabbat services – seeks out the Chumash which was donated in memory of our son Gil, and at the same time seeks out the Chumash of Reb Marvin Hirsch. She brings it to me and says, "Do not forget to give it to Chaim when he arrives."

May Professor Dr. Marvin Hirsch's memory be forever and may his children and grandchildren be able to do Mitzvot in his merit till 120. AMEN!!

Today's Rosh Chodesh!

By Dr. David Epstein

Many years ago, when I was working long shifts in the hospital, it was especially challenging to attend minyan every day, but I made a special effort to come to shul every Sunday and Rosh Chodesh. One Rosh Chodesh morning, I attended shul in usual fashion. Marvin walked in late, as he clearly forgot it was Rosh Chodesh and the minyan would therefore start a few minutes earlier. Upon seeing me, it triggered his memory. He slapped his hand onto his forehead, and said, "I totally forgot, it's Rosh Chodesh!"

I found it quite amusing – and impressive – that Marvin associated my coming to shul with it being either Rosh Chodesh or Sunday. Marvin took interest in people and recognized the Mitzvos they performed, associating them with those Mitzvos. He continues to be missed, but every Rosh Chodesh, I am reminded of what a special person he was.

Picture Perfect

By Dr. Walter Fingerer

There are so many incidental conversations that Marvin and I had over the course of our friendship. However, I will relate a couple of conversations we had, which will reflect, in some small way, the true persona of Marvin Hirsch, O'H.

The first episode deals with preparation for marriage to Corinne. Marvin was more upbeat than usual and smiled from ear to ear when he gave me the wonderful news of their engagement. He assured me I was on the invite list and to save the date. I was thrilled for him and knew that Corinne had to be someone very special since Marvin was so special. I got to the chupah early, as Marvin requested, and he handed me his camera and asked if I knew how to take pictures. I was excited and felt privileged to participate, in any way, in this wonderful simcha. The atmosphere was charged with well wishers and the tone was of extreme happiness for the chassan and kallah. The evening was beautiful and the guests could not contain their joy and enthusiasm for the bride and groom, uniquely meant for each other.

A week or two later, I was invited to see the fruits of my labor. Marvin, in his inimitable way, was so charged with appreciation and enthusiasm with the pictures, that he officially offered me the job of family photographer! I was to be the one to memorialize all future simchas for the Hirsch family. He was true to his word and I became the photographer for Chaim's bris, etc. You see, Marvin was "paying" me by bestowing this honor to be the family photo archivist. He brought me closer to the family, and in his way of thinking, by making me "photographer," I became an ex officio member of his closely knit, loving family. I understood the significance of what he did and over the ensuing years, he brought me closer to his inner thoughts.

A remarkable friendship ensued over the next several years. You see, Marvin had priorities in life, as many of us do. His priorities went something like this: First came Hashem, next his family, and closely behind, k'lal yisrael. He was deeply in love with Corinne, and had great respect for her and her family.

Marvin's kovod expressed to his mom and dad was legendary, and his loyalty to friends and community was unparalleled. In his dealing with friends and strangers, he managed to say little but do much, always greeting people with a cheerful countenance. His affable personality allowed him to intercede between two arguing people and make shalom. He exemplified the quintessential peace maker, loving and running after peace.

During my many visits with him at the hospital, when he was quite ill and in pain, we would have quiet time together. I didn't want to burden him with other people's problems and issues. He would sit up and ask questions about problems other people were experiencing and would then say, "Wally, how can we help?" Here was a man who was terminally ill, in severe pain, and his major concern was to help others get past their "pain." Yes, Marvin loved people, all people of God's creation.

Imbued with his honest love of God, he was able to forge a life filled with care, kindness, respect, and honor for family, friends, and mankind, Jew and non-Jew alike. He was the epitome of a deeply religious man embracing morality and ethics above reproach. In a world of indifference and self indulgence, Marvin brought selflessness, honest friendship, and God into the lives of those who had the privilege of meeting him. To have met Marvin was to get to know him. To get to know him was to love him.

Heeding Counsel

By Miriam Friedman

What more can I say than has already been said about him? He was an exemplary person – good hearted – wonderful to his dear and extended family *and* a really religious Jew.

He took his religion very seriously. In fact, at one point, our principal, Mike DeBellis, remarked: "I hope that's the end of the Jewish holidays for this year." He taught me how to be a good Jew. I followed his teachings and was observant of the holidays, too.

Marvin Hirsch was a great counselor. He instituted Group Counseling at South Junior High School. At one time he had four or five groups meeting in one day. I had all I could do to keep up with so much activity.

Marvin was an outstanding person – kind and understanding – empathetic to all who needed someone who cared what was happening to them. I miss him very much.

"La Chaim!" Old Friend

By Miriam Friedman and Tom McDonough

[Editor's Note: The following were two handwritten letters sent to the Hirsch family by Miriam Friedman and Tom McDonough, two people who worked with Marvin during his career in Brentwood.]

December 26, 1996

Dear Corinne, Chaim, and Miriam,

    Hope you all are well and doing well. I had written to Tom McDonough about Marvin's death in my Christmas greetings to him and the family, and the enclosed is his reply. Everyone loved Marvin for the fine, principled, and upstanding person he was, as evident in Tom's feelings for Marvin, and many others who knew him.

Love,

Miriam Freidman

December 1996

Dear Miriam,

I was saddened to learn of Marvin's death. He was truly a man for all seasons and I considered him a dear friend. Some of my fondest memories of my time in Brentwood center around him and the good times we had. He loved people and I remember one particular time he toasted me with a hearty and heartfelt "La Chaim!" That's how I want to remember him. "La Chaim" old friend, because you lived life to the fullest and have no fear of judgment.

Love,

Tom

Sponsored

By Dr. David Goldberger

I sat next to Marvin and his son, Chaim, virtually every Shabbos afternoon at the weekly Seudah Shlishit (third meal) at the Young Israel of Hollywood-Ft. Lauderdale. During that time, Marvin would constantly talk about finding and recruiting sponsors for Seudah Shlishit, to help raise money for the shul.

He mentioned on several occasions that someone should call people who had Yahrtzeit that week, and encourage them to sponsor Seudah Shlishit in memory of their loved one. I believe Marvin himself made those phone calls for some time, and took a proactive approach in helping the shul.

As one of the early pioneers and members of the Young Israel, Marvin was always looking for ways to assist the shul in any way he could. Even though he frequently felt he was "banging his head against the wall," even a minimal positive response was an important mitzvah on behalf of the shul.

The Garden of Inspiration

By Dr. Norman Goldglantz and Family

In the days towards the end of Marvin's life, I went to visit him in his house. He was very ill, and was attached to an IV on wheels, which sat next to his bed.

In the middle of the visit, Marvin mentioned that he had to go water his plants, tomatoes, and other vegetables in the garden in his backyard! I was stunned, and couldn't believe it. He was sick and practically bedridden, yet he wanted to get up and go water his garden!

I assisted Marvin as he stood up, and as determined as I had ever seen, he marched outside, rolling his IV alongside him. He watered his plants and the rest of the garden, clearly feeling fulfilled that he had taken care of them.

Most people in that position wouldn't care about their garden or plants. But Marvin took great pride in everything he did, and his strength, determination, and willpower was an inspiration for everyone in the community.

From Strength to Strength

By David and Chanu Goldis

Even when Marvin was sick and going all over for treatments, I remember a "gibor" standing at his spot next to the bimah every day, morning and night, for minyan. Never a bad thing to say, and never a complaint about what he was going through. Always a smile and good word.

When he got progressively worse, we at Bikur Cholim set up shifts to be there with him, which I, of course, took one every day. But I also made sure to be there a second time every morning to have the zechus to put Tallis and Tefillin on Marvin. He might have been in pain and not had the strength to daven, but he never refused when I showed up. In retrospect, maybe he did it so I wouldn't feel bad or get upset that I schlepped there and he didn't want to daven. But I thank God that I did have that time with him every day, as I got to hear his wisdom, and a boxing story or two.

I can remember vividly either a nurse or someone else saying to me, "the organization that you volunteer for is wonderful, that you go visit the sick." I said back, "I'm not doing this as a volunteer of Bikur Cholim; this is a good friend who I respect and want to do anything I can to make it easy for him."

The Tehillim Club

By Irwin Gottlieb

Marvin approached me over 15 years ago about joining a Tehillim Club. He told me that his cousin was organizing a Tehillim project, where each person would commit to saying a designated cluster of Tehillim each week. With a combined effort, the entire book of Tehillim would be read each and every week. Marvin was so enthusiastic about it that he even gave me an Artscroll Tehillim to keep, which he inscribed. I still have it to this day and even showed it to his son, Chaim, who immediately recognized his father's handwriting.

Marvin was the type of person who tried to better this world and the people around him. While most people probably had passive roles in this Tehillim Club, Marvin was proactive and took the initiative to make sure the maximum amount of people would be saying Tehillim. There is no doubt that his efforts serve as a long lasting tribute and merit to his name. Until this day, I use it daily to recite my favorite Tehillim every morning. His zest for making yiddishkeit a meaningful experience on a daily basis was an inspiration to all who knew him.

Welcome to Texas

By Ruben N. Gottlieb

Often I have a picture in my mind's eye of Marvin in his yellow Izod sweater and he is smiling as he always did.

I remember a trip I made to Texas about thirteen years ago and I had mentioned it to Marvin. He told me that he had a friend in Texas and asked if I would look him up. I called Marvin's friend and he told me that Marvin had called him and told him that one of his gabboim who was an attorney would be calling him. Marvin had asked him to extend all courtesies to me and help me if I needed anything. This act of chesed touched me so and I don't recall ever thanking Marvin, which I hope I did.

Marvin (and Corinne, I might add) are terrific people. He was the ultimate Mensch and expected nothing in return. He deserved Yariches Yomin (a longer life) but he lives on in the two special children he had. I know Chaim and Miriam are making him proud and that he is looking down at them in his yellow Izod sweater and smiling.

No Stranger to Torah

By Susan Grossman

When I think of Marvin, I see a gentle man, with a distinctive walk, carrying his coat over his arm, always with a sweet, smiling face and a kind word upon his lips. When I first moved to Hollywood, my first Shabbos lunch invitation was from Marvin and Corinne. I felt very awkward but they made me feel right at home. My memories are also of Miriam and Chaim playing in the back yard.

I was just "returning" to Judaism when I moved here. Marvin was always there to answer a question or correct a mistake in a most loving way. I remember that he was the one that was selected to tell my husband and me not to open the trunk of our car in the parking lot on Shabbos to get out prayer books because the light was turning on. And, we were so proud that we were walking! Marvin first suggested that my husband get a locker so that we wouldn't have to open the trunk, and THEN explained the Halachah. Marvin made it okay for us to make mistakes as we "returned."

My other bright memory is seeing Marvin stand beside Chaim, who must have been no older than four, as Chaim said the Torah Brachas on Simchat Torah. That told me everything about Marvin. He was guiding his child in the way of Torah...just like he did strangers.

It is always with a lump in my throat that I recall these memories. I am a better person for having known Marvin, and I continue to reap rewards in my dear friendships with Corinne, Chaim and Miriam. The apple does not fall too far from the tree!

May his neshama have an aliyah!

Kaddish Gadol: Marvin to the Rescue

By Maurice Gruber

About 16 years ago, I was reciting Kaddish Gadol for my dad in the main sanctuary of our shul. Being upset, I lost my concentration and had trouble keeping up with the pace of the other mourners. Marvin, who also was saying Kaddish, was standing to my left at the opposite end of the row. Noticing my dilemma, he slowed down and much to my relief, the two of us were in synch. Thank you, Marvin, for your sensitivity and act of kindness. I was especially proud to recite Kaddish in synch with you.

The Thumb Trick

By Btzalel Hirschhorn

Towards the end when Marvin was too sick to come to shul on Shabbos, after the early minyan, we would come over to the house with a group of other people to visit him.

I used to sit next to him on the couch and he would show me the little trick where he would put his thumb in between his pinky and his fourth finger on one hand, and on the other, he would tuck his thumb all the way underneath his other fingers and curl the fingers over his thumb. Then, he would put one hand on top of the other, and then quickly pull his two hands apart, giving the magical allusion that he was pulling his thumb apart. I remember I could never figure out how he did it. He used to also tell me rhymes (and songs, too).

Despite the fact I was only about ten years old when he passed away, I still have those memories of him and we all really loved him. I am sure that from the Maasim Tovim done for him, his neshama is having a tremendous Aliyah.

We're Here to Talk About You

By Tevi Hirschhorn

Marvin's memory will always be clear in my mind. He was a very special person. One thing that really stood out in my mind, which I will never forget, was Marvin's unceasing efforts to make others feel good, even towards the end of his illness and pain.

I came by to visit him one Shabbos afternoon to see how he was doing. I don't remember how far along he was in his illness, but he was already bed-ridden, and on oxygen. I remember stopping in and asking Corinne how he was doing, and she said he was not doing well today and was not seeing visitors. She said she would go in and ask him if he was up to seeing me, anyway.

She returned a few moments later and said he was very happy I came and would be glad to see me. When I came in the room, he was all smiles and full of cheer. He asked how I was doing and what I was doing; how school was going and how my parents and siblings were. He was very interested and excited to see me, and I remember leaving the room feeling really happy. I was young and easily distracted back then, and it was only a few minutes later that I realized I hadn't even talked about how he was feeling! He wouldn't even let me start and dove right into talking about me and making me feel good. I completely forgot what I had come there to do!

He was so selfless and full of love for others that he would not dwell on his own pain or feel sorry for himself. He was committed to kindness and humility, and would not be deterred from that path.

Sun Birds

By Dr. Naphtali Hoffman

I remember Marvin well. Every summer, the Hirsch family would flock from Hollywood, Florida to Elmira, New York, to visit Corinne's parents, Paul and Hennie Sall. I always looked forward to the Hirsch visits to Elmira so I could spend some time with my pal Marvin. There was a distinct shortage of Bnei Torah in Elmira, particularly in my age group.

I can remember swinging by the Sall house every morning to pick up Marvin for minyan, and again every night for the evening services. It is hard to believe we managed to sustain a minyan for so many years, but we did.

I also remember sitting on the Sall's front porch, drinking pitchers of ice tea and snacking on fruit and cake. Marvin and I used to trade stories about our students and colleges, occasionally complain about some things, and even learn a little bit too (which is what we were supposed to be doing all along). For some reason, we never talked about politics, so we agreed about almost everything. Marvin was a really funny guy, and very well informed as well.

I also remember visiting him in Florida at his home the year he died. We both knew we would never see each other again, but managed not to talk about it. We actually had a great time together, as we always did. I miss him very much.

All Men Are Not Created Equal

By Benyamin Israel

When I moved to Hollywood, Florida in 1981, I immediately met Marvin and his family. I have very fond memories of Marvin, as he was personable and was always looking to help others. He was pleasant, always had a smile on his face, and was constantly trying to help people.

Although it didn't materialize, Marvin wanted me to take a course at Heed University. Marvin was passionate about his school, and it showed in his daily conversations with everyone.

We would talk about boxing, as we both had an interest in the sport. When we were young, each of us did recreational boxing, so it was a topic we often discussed. We would muse about famous boxing rivals, such as Willie Pep and Sandy Sadler.

It wasn't until years later that Marvin and I discovered we grew up very close to one another in Brooklyn. I lived on Melrose Street, and he lived on Teneyck Walk in Williamsburg, New York. It was ironic that we had lived so close to one another, but never knew each other until we both moved to Florida.

I did some carpentry work for the Hirsch's at their home on 49th Avenue, both for their shed in the backyard and the lattice that was used as the Hirsch's Succah each year.

Marvin was always in attendance at shul during the week. You could count on Marvin to be there for davening every morning and evening, as well as attending classes and shiurim.

In good nature, I would encourage Marvin to stop smoking, and he would, in good nature, tell me how hard it was for him to stop. I appreciated his valiant efforts and understood how challenging it was for him.

Some years later, when I had my own radio show, Marvin was very supportive of my efforts. He was a frequent caller, injecting the show with stimulating ideas and good thoughts to build upon.

We had a great relationship. Marvin was quite a guy. They say that "all men are created equal." But when you met a man like Marvin Hirsch, you knew he was in a class above the rest. It was a delight to know him.

Welcoming Party

By Dr. Mark Jaffe

My family and I moved to Hollywood, Florida in the summer of 1995. I walked into the Young Israel of Hollywood-Ft. Lauderdale as a stranger in a new shul. The first person to approach me was Marvin. He came over, introduced himself, and welcomed me to the community. The conversation continued as Marvin asked where we were living. When I informed him of the block we were on, he suddenly got very excited, and passionately said, "Wow, we're right down the street – we're neighbors!" I was amazed at the genuine enthusiasm and excitement Marvin had for welcoming a new member into the community – someone he had never met before.

As time went on, I observed Marvin welcoming other new people into the community. I realized the warm welcome was embedded in his demeanor and personality. He truly greeted everyone with an incredible sense of Hachnasas Orchim (hospitality). It was almost as if Marvin was uncomfortable knowing there was someone new in town who did not receive a warm welcome.

One of Chaim's memories is how I stopped off at the Hirsch household on Friday night after davening. I came simply to schmooze with the family and get an update on how Marvin was feeling (and see the family dog, a French poodle whom I nicknamed "Fifi").

While I only knew Marvin for the last couple years of his life, it was clear that his welcoming attitude and friendly personality were the essence of who he was. Now almost thirteen years later, I still haven't forgotten who the first person was that came up to me.

The Role Model Around the Corner

By Tammy Landa and Family

Whenever I think of Marvin, I immediately remember his infectious smile. He was a giant, yet truly humble and quiet in the way he conducted himself. He didn't show off his knowledge or deeds, but was truly great in stature. Marvin never thought of himself; instead, he always thought of others. He accepted everyone and never looked down on anyone.

I especially remember how Marvin acted as a father-figure to my two boys, Baruch and Bentzion. The boys loved to see Marvin's famous finger trick, where he would magically slide his thumb "on and off." They looked to him as a role model and when they went to shul, they would often sit next to Marvin. He had an amazing bond and connection with the children in the community. It's no surprise the children were drawn to him, as he was righteous, brilliant, soft spoken, and never had a bad word to say about anyone.

Marvin had such a big heart and gave himself to the community. He did an amazing amount of Chesed – both for our family and the community. I'll never be able to repay him for his kindness, but will always remember and cherish everything he did. Marvin was greater than life – a true Tzaddik.

Towards the end of his life, I was humbled when Corinne asked me to be Marvin's nurse and assist in administering some of his shots. I was honored that the Hirsch's felt close enough to ask for my help. Every time I went to the Hirsch home, it lit up my world, and I looked for opportunities to come back. I truly felt part of the family.

Marvin's will to live was so strong, as evidenced by his love for family, where he gave of himself time and time again. Marvin never lost sight of life. His spirits were upbeat even in the most trying times and were a small glimpse into the special personality of Marvin Hirsch.

The Russian War Colonel, Demitri Draguten

By Marc Levine

In the history of the South Florida Jewish community, I recall only a handful of people that had an everlasting impact on the entire neighborhood. Marvin Hirsch is at the top of this list.

Though I hadn't developed a very close relationship with Marvin, there are several specific interactions he and I had that remind me of his friendly smile and his mastery of kindness. In general, to say the least, his warm and embracing personality made me feel like we were best friends every time we saw each other, though it often went beyond the warm smile and friendly disposition. Marvin seemed genuinely interested in what I was doing in my life and he regularly offered an amusing opinion and at times some good advice.

When I was thirteen years old and aspiring to be the next David Copperfield, Marvin took note of my interests in performing magic and illusions. He visited my house unannounced one evening with a dark green book in his hand (the cover of which had seen better days). The book he had come to lend me was simply titled "Houdini." It was the first book I had ever read about the legendary magician, and as Marvin predicted, the stories only inspired me to pursue my talents even more. He would also challenge me to learn the tricks that were included in an underutilized magic trick set he once bought for Chaim as a birthday gift. He authentically appreciated my passion and made it his selfless duty to inject some excitement into my hobby. I still practice today.

Marvin was also known to have an ongoing personal "schtick" with several people in the community. I don't recall what lead to the dialogue Marvin and I often had, but it was always fun to play along. Marvin had a delightful fixation with a particular Russian War Colonel, Demitri Draguten. Perhaps it was the name that was simply fun to say, but it was always amusing listening to Marvin roll the name off his tongue in a well faked Russian accent. It was naturally accompanied with a salute. Marvin and I would greet each other by standing at attention, saluting one another and exclaiming "Colonel Demitri Draguten" in unison.

When it was time to go Marvin would never walk away without a good thumb wrestle match. In my early teenage years I thought "Hey, I'm in my prime – I could take him." Little did I know Marvin was a well experienced thumb wrestling champion (if there were such a sport I have no doubt he'd be a title holder). It was always fun and I think he even let me win…once.

The Tree of Life

By Norman Levine

When our family moved here in 1989, one of the first couples we met were Marvin and Corinne, who lived around the block from us. In one of my first encounters with Marvin, he took me into his backyard, and proudly showed me a tree house he had been working on for Chaim and Miriam to play in. Marvin was so excited and proud that he had put this tree house together for his children, and was beaming ear to ear. Marvin and Corinne invited us for a Shabbos meal on one of our first weeks in Hollywood, and we quickly saw how he loved his family.

Marvin constantly joked that he and I should go into business together. He had an entrepreneurial spirit, with great enthusiasm in everything he did. He was filled with passion and excitement, as he would ritually come up with new and innovative ideas.

In subsequent years, I attended the 7 AM early minyan on Shabbos morning. Virtually every week, there was a sit-down Kiddush, and Chaim would give a short Dvar Torah. Every week, I would look over at Marvin when Chaim was speaking, and without needing to say anything, Marvin just nodded, smiled, and got pure nachas from hearing his son speak.

Marvin cherished his family and loved every moment he had with them. Marvin was one of the most loved members of this community and when we lost him, everybody felt the loss. In life, it is rare that you come across a person about whom nobody has a bad word to say. Marvin was one of those people. He is missed to this day. I'll always remember his friendly nature and his warm smile which seemed to be permanently in tow at all times. Even at the end, he never lost his Marvin personality.

A Dreamer With a Winning Smile

By Dr. Gary Magid

I have two distinct memories of Marvin, both qualities of which were hallmarks of his personality. The first is that Marvin was a dreamer. Some people are afraid to dream – but Marvin Hirsch was not one of them. He loved to come up with new ideas, goals, and projects. I remember him as someone who was innovative and creative, always looking to improve things. Many people shy way from dreaming and don't pursue their goals, but I respected and admired Marvin for being one of those who constantly dreamed and aspired to move higher.

The second memory I have of Marvin was his larger-than-life smile. He was always beaming about something – whether it was his family, community, or simply another good idea that had just come to him. He always greeted people warmly with a big grin, and truly exemplified Pirkei Avos when it says (1:15) "Receive every person with a cheerful and pleasant countenance."

An Intuition for Torah Education

By Rabbi Chaim Mandel

I remember Marvin when he was already diagnosed with the illness that ultimately took him from us. But my memory is one of a strong-willed individual with what seemed to be boundless energy.

While deeply rooted in education his whole life, he had a keen intuition that the Yeshiva and Bais Yakov were the right places for his children. He had a love of life and an enthusasm for giving and teaching, which resonated deep within me. May his memory be a blessing for the entire family.

Repeat Performance

By Richard Mayer

I would like to share a short memory of Marvin that resonates his devotion to his family. I remember being at Young Israel a long time ago, and at the time, the whole place and experience was new to me. But I remember a beautiful thing that stayed with me until today. There was this kind, happy man there. He had two little kids with him: an adorable red-haired boy and his little sister. He was so devoted to them, and they were equally attached to him.

Recently, when Chaim asked me to share and document my memories of Marvin, I was emotionally moved by his motives, compiling stories and memories about his father so future generations will know who Marvin was. "I want my kids to hear about my father through other people's perspective," Chaim explained. Repeat performance.

"Hearty Appetite, Esquire"

By Heshie and Joan Niad

In the late 1970's, we spent Rosh Hashanah at the Seagull Hotel in Miami Beach. Also staying at the hotel was Marvin, his parents, and brother. We had a wonderful time with the Hirsch family over Rosh Hashanah, and observed Marvin's respectful, dignified, and warm disposition.

We recall how Marvin interacted with Joan's father, Mr. Gottlieb, who was an accomplished attorney. When sitting down to eat dinner, Marvin would say to Mr. Gottlieb, "Hearty appetite, Esquire" (and sometimes using the alternate "Counselor" instead of "Esquire"), as a way of honoring and showing respect. At the time, Marvin was proudly starting Heed University, and in response, my father would consciously reply, "Hearty appetite as well, Counselor." It was beautiful to observe how they both admired and paid tribute to one another.

We also remember a short while later, when meeting Corinne for the first time, Marvin's proud and excited demeanor when introducing Corinne to his friends. He would jokingly ask, "Do you know where she's from? Elmira, New York – do you know where Elmira is?"

Years later, when Marvin was working as a Mashgiach at a deli in Coral Springs, we often came up for dinner. Upon seeing us, he would come out from the kitchen, come over to our table, and say something to the effect of, "the Chinese is excellent this week," or, "the mushroom barley soup is really good" and then wish us a "hearty appetite." Joan's dad was long gone by then, but Marvin remembered the phrase from years earlier, and was his way of telling us how dearly he remembered him. Marvin was always warm and friendly, a trademark of who he was.

We lived in the same community as the Hirsch family for over two decades, and will always remember Marvin for his respect and admiration he showed to people.

A Small, But Meaningful, Chesed

By Lewis Niad

In the early days of the shul, Marvin was proactive in setting up the Seudah Shlishit (third meal on Shabbos) for the shul. He would put out the rolls, tuna fish, drinks, and other miscellaneous food that was in the kitchen. Years ago, in the early 1990's, Marvin approached me and mentioned that he thought the catering for the Seudah Shlishit needed some improvement.

Knowing that I was in the catering business, he asked if I would be interested in taking on the responsibility of being the caterer for Seudah Shlishit, and subsequently asked the Rabbi for his approval as well. For many years to follow, I catered the Seudah Shlishit at the shul, and it all stemmed from Marvin's initial probing.

While it was a logical fit, and a relatively small chesed, I greatly appreciated that he thought of me. Even a small chesed can make a significant impact on a person for years to come – which was a sign of who Marvin was.

Let's Dance!

By Rabbi Mordechai Palgon

I arrived in Miami in August 1994. New town, new job, new people. My first interactions with certain people left indelible imprints on my memory which will last a lifetime. One such person was Dr. Marvin Hirsch A"H. He embraced every project which we undertook here in the Yeshiva with the enthusiasm of a little boy in an ice cream parlor. He encouraged, praised and at times, would even give a little fatherly "slap on the back" as an added measure of that encouragement.

One such incident I recall was during my first year of teaching his son, Chaim h"b. We had completed Mishnayos Makos and I wanted to make a big deal out of it. Unsure as to the degree of parental support that would be forthcoming, I called Marvin. He jumped for joy – his son had finished a mesechta! He told me to go all out, get a band, make a sit-down meal and invite all the parents. "Let's dance!" he shouted enthusiastically. Then, he sent a check to cover much of the anticipated expense.

I was inspired! I called my Rabbeim in New York to inquire regarding the acceptable protocol for a siyum on Mishnayos. Typically, siyumim are reserved for the completion of an entire tractate of Gemorah or a full seder (section) of Mishnayos. The p'sak I received astounded me. Eighth graders finishing a mesechta of Mishnayos should be treated with the esteem and pomp of a full-fledged siyum. Additionally, it was advised that we recite the hadran (the concluding prayer which is the basis for the siyum).

The p'sak was said over in the name of HaGaon HaRav Moshe Feinstein ZT"L, the preeminent posek of the generation. He said that young boys need to feel they are "bar siyumim" – students who are capable of finishing projects. Therefore, we should be prepared to go all out, so to speak, to convey this message, as well as the Yeshiva's pride in them for this accomplishment.

Dr. Hirsch did not hold himself to be a Torah scholar by any stretch. Yet, he had the yashrus (straightness of thought) and wisdom of the greatest Torah scholar! He clearly knew what to stand up for and when to do it. I remember that siyum as clearly as if it were yesterday. I remember Chaim saying over one of the mishnayos. And, of course, I remember right after the hadran was recited, listening to the liebidig music that was being played by Chaim's classmate, Eli Riesel. I made my way over to Marvin Hirsch. He thrust out his hand to me and said, "Rabbi Palgon, let's DANCE!!"

THAT was Marvin; that was his gadlus. How very fortunate I was to have had the z'chus of knowing him.

Yehi zichroh baruch.

The Honor is Mine

By Abe Saada

Marvin was a very touching person. He was humble in everything he said and did. However, the trait I remember most about Marvin was the way he treated his mother – it was with the utmost of respect and honor. He would carry her on his shoulders if he was capable. It was touching to observe the Kibbud (respect) and loyalty he showed to his mother. Although I never met Marvin's father, he would always talk about him as well, as someone who was influential and impacted his life.

Marvin loved Judaism, and I remember going with him to many classes and Shiurim at Heed University. Marvin made sure to incorporate Torah learning into his work-day by welcoming Rabbi's to Heed University to deliver weekly classes.

I remember visiting Marvin in the hospital several times in his last weeks, and his dedication to Judaism, his mother, and the rest of the family was remarkable, even as Hashem took him too soon from this world.

Better than Mr. Rogers

By Dr. Islon and Eve Seliger

Marvin Hirsch was a unique person, radiating with warmth and care. He treated young and old alike with respect. The many hours he spent with our son, Ronen, were invaluable; he was Ronen's "Mr. Rogers," only far superior! He was always cheerful, interesting, and interested in those around him. He never complained, even towards the end, when he was suffering and in pain. It was a privilege to have Marvin as a friend and neighbor.

The Little Boccherini Fan

By Ronen Seliger

As a young boy I recall fond memories of a man I knew as Mr. Shersh, or as everyone else knew him, Marvin Hirsch. When I was a toddler, the Hirsch's were our neighbors. I would leave my house, often without even telling my mother, and go to my next door neighbors for some daily enlightenment.

As I would sip my juice and eat my snack, Mr. Shersh, as I lovingly referred to him, would give me my daily dose of the renowned composer of classical music, Luigi Boccherini. We would sit there and Mr. Shersh would give me a brief history lesson on who Boccherini was and what type of music we were listening to. With each passing day, I grew to appreciate Boccherini for what he really symbolized to me – spending time with a man who was like a surrogate father to me.

He was remarkable in that he transcended age and bridged a generation gap. He made me feel important and special as he patiently opened a whole new world of music to me. I will always cherish and value the special time we shared together. Mr. Shersh, as I will always remember him, was truly a righteous man.

Relationships from Coast to Coast

By Rabbi Howard and Dena Seif

My memories of the Hirsch family date back to the 1970's in Los Angeles, where I first met the family. Later becoming reacquainted in Hollywood, Florida, I always remember Marvin with a large smile on his face. He was jubilant and sustained a happy-go-lucky attitude.

Many years ago, I recall stopping off weekly at the Hirsch home on my way back from Shul after Friday night davening, just to schmooze with the family. I did this for quite some time, and enjoyed the welcoming atmosphere created by Marvin and Corinne.

On a separate occasion, I arrived home from Shul one Friday night with all the children – except one. Dena asked about the whereabouts of our son, Solly, and after looking around behind me and realizing he wasn't with the rest of the children, I went to go find him. As I walked around the corner, there was Marvin walking with Solly, guiding him home. Marvin noticed Solly inadvertently separated from the rest of the family, and made sure to escort him across the busy streets and back home safely. Marvin was always aware and took notice of situations such as these, always looking to help where he could.

When Marvin's mother, Ida, was ill, Marvin would ask me to visit her in order to cheer her up. I always respected Marvin for doing everything he could to improve his mother's physical and emotional health. In Marvin's later years, he asked me to walk to a local hospital during Rosh Hashanah, where his mom was recovering from surgery. Marvin was not physically able to walk far distances at that time, yet wanted his mother to hear the Shofar on Rosh Hashanah. I admired his dedication and care to his mother, combined with his care and concern of mitzvah performance.

A Devoted Son, Husband, and Father

By Lynette Sookdeo

My name is Lynette Sookdeo and I came to America from Trinidad in 1994. I am a home health care nurse's aid. The first patient I had was a lovely lady named Ida Hirsch. I met Ida's son, Marvin, and believe me, he was a wonderful, loyal, and devoted person. I wish every mother would have a son like Marvin. He was so good to his mother. Not only was he good to his mother, but also a very good husband, father, and brother.

I cared for Ida from evening until the next morning. There were times I would spend Shabbos with Ida at Marvin's house. Marvin and Corinne treated me so nicely and always made me feel welcome.

Although Marvin was sick himself, he never complained of his own pain and suffering. He would come to see his mother every morning after he went to shul. Marvin would stay and take care of his mother while I went home for a few hours.

I began caring for Marvin when his illness got worse in 1996. He always treated me with the utmost respect and like a member of his own family. He was so kind and gentle. No matter how sick Marvin was, he was still concerned about others.

I have three sons and I would want them to treat me the way Marvin treated his mother.

Summer Learning

By Daniel Stahl

In the summer of 1993, I was approached by Marvin Hirsch with a simple request. His son, Chaim, was about to enter the seventh grade at Yeshiva Toras Chaim in the fall, and Marvin wanted Chaim to learn with me throughout that summer. As I worked in Toras Chaim, and had the summer off, Marvin thought that it would be an excellent preparation for Chaim to have that extra learning in the summer.

I had met Marvin and Chaim years earlier when I first started going to the Young Israel of Hollywood, where I used to see Marvin every day at Shacharis and Mincha, very often with little Chaim nearby. Soon afterwards, I moved to a home within a block or so of the Hirsch home, and, as well as becoming close neighbors, we also became close friends.

I gladly agreed to Marvin's request. Chaim and I learned throughout that summer, very often with Marvin joining us. Little did Marvin know that what started as a summer learning session was to evolve into an ongoing Shabbos morning learning seder. For the next several years, Chaim and I learned Mishnah Berurah and Gemora every Shabbos morning after the early minyan, for two to three hours at a time. We even held a siyum on Meseches Megillah at the Yeshiva.

All the years of learning that Chaim and I did together came about because of a simple reason. It was the request of a loving father, whose dedication to his family and love of Torah and Torah learning clearly guided his actions. He wanted his love of Torah to be passed on to his children, but rather than sit back passively and hope that it would happen, he did what had to be done to ensure its success. As a neighbor, friend, and a source of inspiration, Marvin will always be missed, but his merits continue to live on.

Agent 86

By Miguel Stahl

One of the things that stands out the most in my mind about Marvin, besides his gentle, friendly nature was his sense of humor. Even when his physical condition was declining, I remember he always remained positive, and his sense of humor never let up.

He was a fan of the old TV show "Get Smart," as was I. The main character was Maxwell Smart, also known as Secret Agent 86. Well, Marvin started calling me 86, and I'd call him 86 back. He actually wrote me a funny note with stickers on it saying "Top Secret" and "For Your Eyes Only," which he addressed as being from 86 to Agents 1 and 86, meaning myself and my brother Danny. This was just one example of how Marvin was friendly, outgoing, and created a special bond with people that had personal warmth and meaning.

Just a couple of years ago, our friend Channock, who had done air conditioning work at the Hirsch's house years earlier, mentioned what a nice guy my neighbor was. I asked him which neighbor, and he told me he couldn't remember his name.

He said, "You know, 86."

I knew exactly who he was talking about.

Marvin Hirsch: A True Mentsh

By Miriam Stahl

We were privileged to meet Marvin and his beautiful family when we moved to this community. Marvin and Corinne welcomed us with a beautiful sponge cake, which they brought for our first Shabbat. "Here, for your Shabbat – enjoy!" Corinne said. "We are your neighbors across the street." It was the beginning of a wonderful friendship.

We were together many times, especially on Shabbat Shiurim. We learned, we talked, and Marvin loved to talk about his pride and joy – his beautiful accomplished children. He was always kind, sweet, and cheerful. I never heard him say a bad word about anyone.

When his mother, A"H was spending Shabbat in their house, we could see the love and respect they all gave her. What an example to their children!

Ahavat Hashem, Ahavat Israel, chesed, and midot tovot all describe Marvin Hirsch, a gentle neshama who left a beautiful legacy to his children to pass to his grandchildren.

He will live forever in the hearts of his family and friends that he loved so much, and who will remember him always lovingly.

In the zechut of his mitzvos and ma'asim tovim, may Hashem bless his beautiful family with good health, hatzlacha, and Shalom.

Close Relationships

By Dr. Nelson and Sheila Stark

It is with great pleasure that we write a story about our family's relationship with Marvin Hirsch.

My family is from Perth Amboy, New Jersey and our Rabbi there was Albert Schwartz and his wife Gloria. Our families were always very close in New Jersey and when we all ended up in South Florida, we maintained that closeness. My wife Sheila then met Rabbi Schwartz while volunteering at South Florida state hospital, through the chaplaincy department.

My wife and I met Marvin at the Young Israel of Hollywood-Ft. Lauderdale in its early days. We started talking about our families and eventually, Rabbi and Mrs. Schwartz's name came up. It was at that time that we realized we had a very special and loving connection with Marvin – since he was Mrs. Schwartz's cousin. Soon after that, in 1985, my wife and I were married. We felt close to Marvin and his family from the very first moment, and cherish the many years of friendship we had with him and his family.

An Educational in Torah

By Raphael Tennenhaus

In the early 1980's, I used to give a Torah class at the homes of Dr. Sam Rand and Sam Schachter. I remember Marvin as being one of the early Torah pioneers in Hollywood. He was one of the first to attend the classes and soak up the words of Torah.

Marvin took pride in his school, Heed University. He encouraged me to get my doctorate from his school, and even though I did not attend, I appreciated his enthusiasm and excitement about his creation.

I recall attending Chaim's upsherin, where his parents were so proud and animated about the special occasion. Marvin was a wonderful person who embraced Torah and education. He made a lasting impression that I remember nearly three decades later.

Come on Down!

By Dr. David Tepper

My best recollection of Marvin Hirsch is that of his smiling face. He embodies the quality from the Mishnah which asks us to greet all people with a pleasant face.

In the summer of 1992, I moved from New York to Hollywood, Florida. As a New Yorker, this was perceived as a major trek in the boonies. No sooner did we arrive at the Young Israel of Hollywood, we realized that we indeed had not left home.

Making our transition that much easier was Marvin Hirsch. I am certain everyone was treated by him with the same dignity and respect. His warmth exuded such that it seemed as if he had a glow about him. For me, however, he represented something in addition: we were landsleit, both of us having come from the Bronx.

He always had a kind word to say and it was spoken and delivered softly, with the utmost sincerity. This is the Dr. Marvin Hirsch I cherish and will always remember – a kind gentle soul who cared for those around him.

My Pal Marvin

By Dr. David Tuchinsky

Marvin Hirsch had incredible Chein – grace – in everything he did. Everyone was important to him, regardless of their heritage, Torah learning level, social or economic background. He displayed a true love of all people, which is very rare. He had an incredible sense of humility when dealing with others. True humility is not thinking less of yourself, but rather more of others – and Marvin displayed that in all his actions.

Marvin represented the mitzvah of Panim Yafos – a happy face – by greeting everyone with a smile or laugh. He always thought in the positive, looking at the glass half full. When he encountered obstacles – whether they were health or otherwise – he inspired others with his laugh and positive attitude.

Marvin loved to hear of other people's simchas and good tidings. He had a special character trait where he would only look at the good in others. He never put his problems on other people and never complained of any troubles. He was a Tzadik and an example of true greatness.

Over twenty years ago, when the shul was small and in its infancy stage, Marvin would help make breakfast after the Sunday morning Minyan. This was just one of the many examples of Marvin's loving personality.

When our son Noah was in first grade, he would go to the Hirsch house to study and review his school materials with Chaim. One of the highlights on Noah's excursion was that Marvin would assist Noah with his reading Hebrew by reciting Tehillim with him.

Marvin had a love of life, and it wasn't limited to people. He loved anything that involved nature, as was clear from his tomato garden in his back yard. I wanted to have a garden just like Marvin's, but didn't know where to begin. Marvin accompanied me to a local store and helped pick out the right tomato plants to start my own garden. He loved to create and grow things, bringing them to life.

Marvin exemplified and mirrored the image of Avrohom Avinu by welcoming people into his home and entertaining them, telling them stories and jokes.

That was Marvin. He was a special person who had a love of Torah, mitzvos, people, and had an incredible sense of grace with everything he did. I called Marvin my "Pal" and will always remember him as that special individual.

An Inspiring Pair of Tefillin

By Yacov Wallerstein

About 13 years ago, I was in Los Angeles on a business trip. I was leaving the jewelry district in downtown Los Angeles, and noticed a few men in a car watching me. Driving through the local streets in LA, I stopped at a gas station on my way to the airport. It was there that I noticed the same car that I had seen back in downtown. Presumably, they were thieves following me in an attempt to rob me. I immediately left the gas station and headed to the airport.

When I was going through the security checkpoint, I put my carry-on bags onto the conveyor belt, and the last bag I put through contained my Tallis and Tefillin. Unfortunately, the thieves stole the last bag which had my Tallis and Tefilin. I was quite upset, as I had been wearing those Tefillin since my Bar Mitzvah.

At that time in 1995, I was in the midst of the year of mourning for my mother. I went to shul the next morning in Hollywood without my Tallis and Tefillin. When I arrived at shul, I noticed a pair of Tefillin on a shelf off to the side, but didn't know who they belonged to. I asked around, but nobody seemed to know. Finally, one of the Gabbaim finally said to just put them on, as they wanted me to lead the davening since I was saying Kaddish for my mother. I put on the Tefillin and began leading the services.

About 15 minutes into the davening, Marvin walked into shul, holding a book on sharks and cancer (which I would later understand was part of a shark cartilage experimental medication he was exploring as a potential cure for cancer). Marvin started looking for his Tefillin and was becoming increasing distraught and frustrated as he continued to search for them in vain. It was at a point in davening where I could not talk, but I finally motioned to him that I had unknowingly put on his Tefillin and was currently wearing them. The look of relief on Marvin's face was amazing when he realized where his Tefillin were.

After we finished davening and were able to talk, he approached me and asked what happened. I explained how my Tallis and Tefillin were stolen the day earlier in Los Angeles, and I was in a frantic and desperate search for some extra Tefillin in order to lead the davening and say Kaddish for my mother. At that point, Marvin gave me a big hug, and said, "Saying Kaddish for your mother is the most important thing; don't worry about taking my Tefillin."

Probably without realizing it, Marvin taught me an incredible lesson. Marvin was towards the end of his life, undergoing pain and suffering from his illness, but he didn't take that bitterness out on other people. He could have yelled and gotten upset at me for taking his Tefillin, but he understood the situation, and had a refreshing perspective on how to handle it. I can only hope that more people learn the lesson of how to interact with others when they are in the midst of their own challenges. Marvin was a role model who is dearly missed.

Willing the Power to Live

By Dr. Neal and Bonnie Weinreb

When I recall Marvin Hirsch, of blessed memory, it is always in the context of good fellowship (meqabbel kol adam b'sever panim yafot – receiving all people with a pleasant face), ahavat yisrael v'kol habriyot – love of Israel and all of God's creations, and above all, quiet but fierce determination and unwavering faith.

I still picture the scene on Shabbat, a few days before his death, when, because he was too weak to walk to shul, we gathered a minyan at his home. He looked barely awakened, yet, nevertheless, he somehow, with Chaim's help, summoned the strength to answer Amen, even rise with a smile to an Aliyah, before nodding off again.

I think that I had the privilege of layning for that minyan. The scroll itself was small and positioned disadvantageously on a low table making it hard for us to see easily. Retrospectively, that seems fortuitous because, maybe that Shabbat, the true message of Torah was in Marvin and not on the parchment.

Marvin was saying Kaddish for his mother, who had just recently died a few months earlier. I can still hear him saying Kaddish, my mind thinking that he had to know he was also saying Kaddish for himself. I still marvel and tremble at the inner strength it must have taken to express absolute acceptance of Hashem's will. I know that moment was the closest I have come to an act of pure Kiddush Hashem.

For years, based I am sure on the religious imperative, v'nishmartem me'od et nishmothaihem and bitahon baSHEM, Marvin resisted medical suggestions that additional treatment of his illness would be futile, and he underwent all sorts of painful, heroic, and experimental procedures with the conviction that abandonment of hope was tantamount to loss of faith. Undoubtedly, he was sustained in this stubborn determination by his love for his family and their reciprocal devotion to him. I never heard him issue a word of despair or even a solitary complaint about his lot in life.

Rabbi Davis recently talked about how he was impacted by people who were called to open the Aron Kodesh on Yom Kippur for the holy prayer, U'netaneh Tokef. I can still see Marvin in his kittel up on the Bimah for this prayer on either his last Rosh Hashanah or Yom Kippur in this world. Then and now, in my mind, it was as if Rabbi Amnon himself had returned for an encore. There are some people whose essence, like Hashem, is not best expressed in bombastic thunder, lightening and wind, but rather in less flamboyant, soft and pleasant tones. Those are the individuals who are the best educators and whose words and actions we should heed the most. Marvin was one of those special people. Even after these many years, we miss him.

Remembering Marvin

By Charlie Zablotsky

I remember the conversations Marvin and I had about higher education and specifically, his founding and work with Heed University. We talked about Franconia College, my alma matter, and how similar the two colleges were in their attention to the importance of individualized education. I believe Marvin also knew the brother of our president at St. Johns in the Virgin Islands. It was refreshing to talk with Marvin, as he was so passionate about education.

At the Young Israel of Hollywood-Ft. Lauderdale, his seat was near mine, and we would also talk about other things (before and after davening, of course!). I distinctly remember that he never had anything bad to say about anyone or anything. He always had a wonderful, jovial, and energetic smile, and when he asked, "how are you," he looked in my eyes and I knew he really meant it.

Family Tree

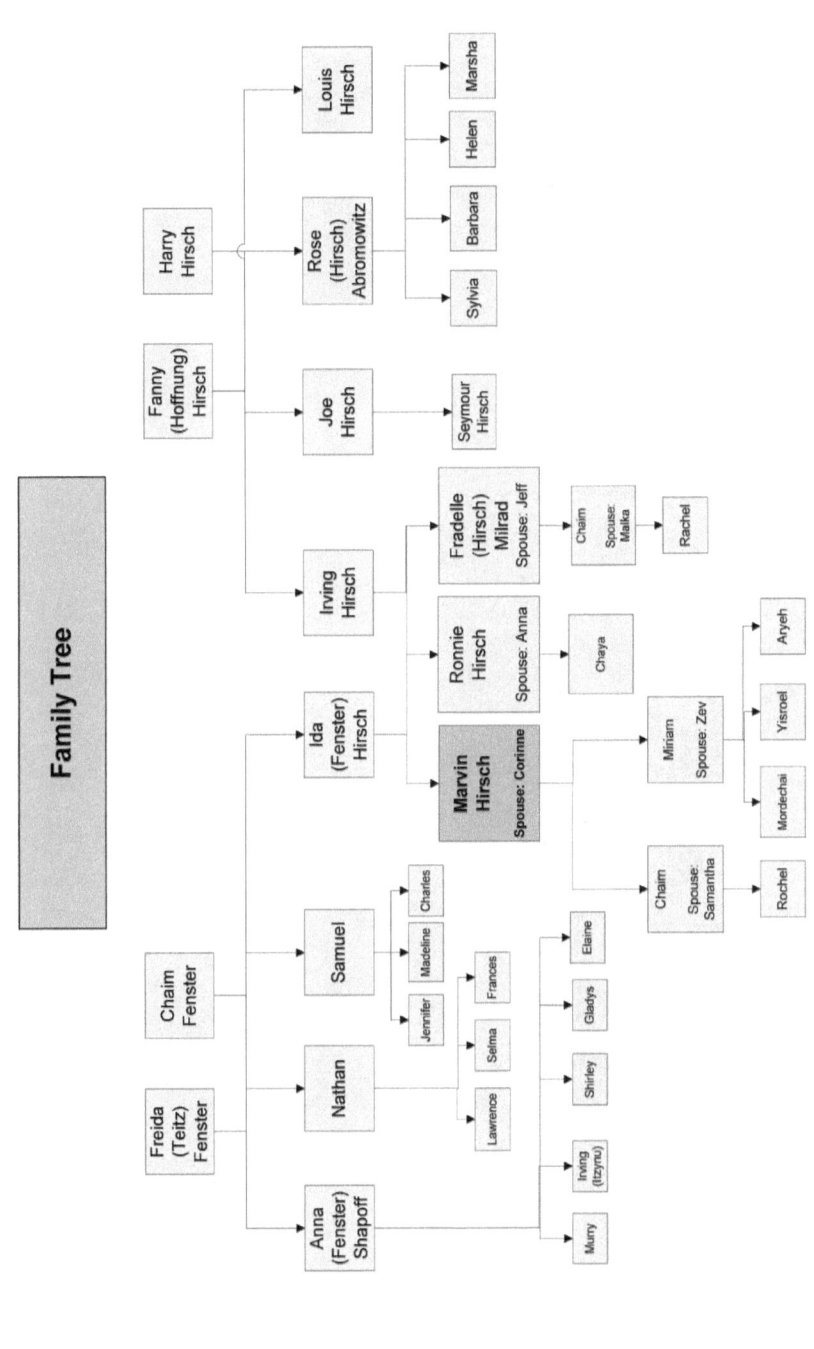

Timeline

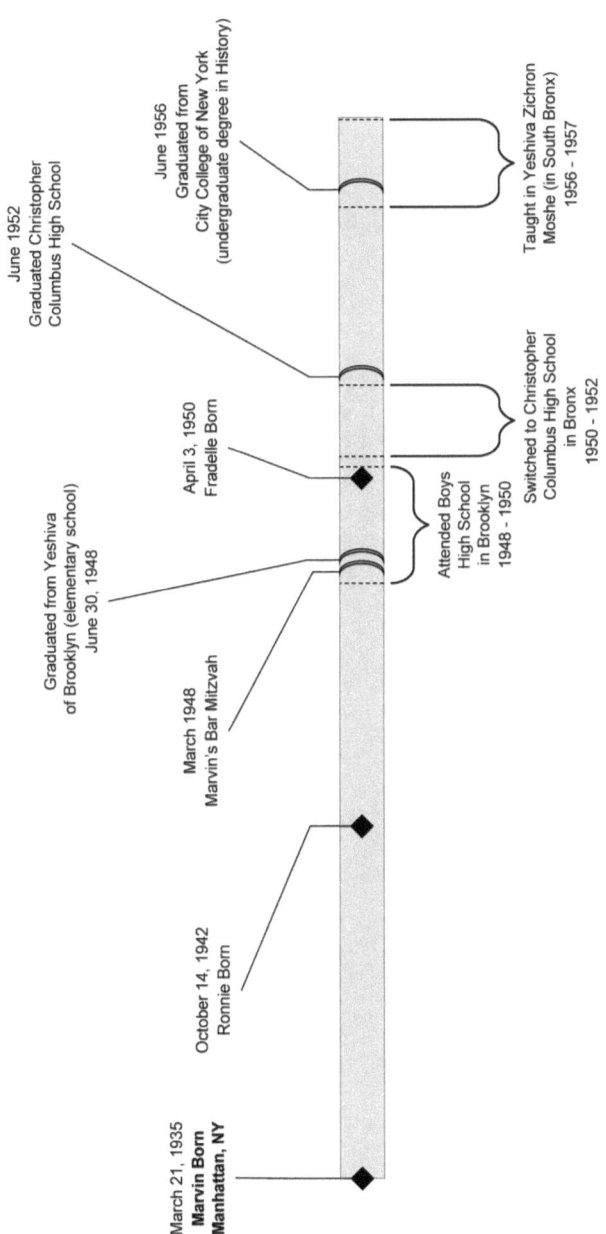

Timeline
Dr. Marvin Hirsch
Part II: 1957 – 1978

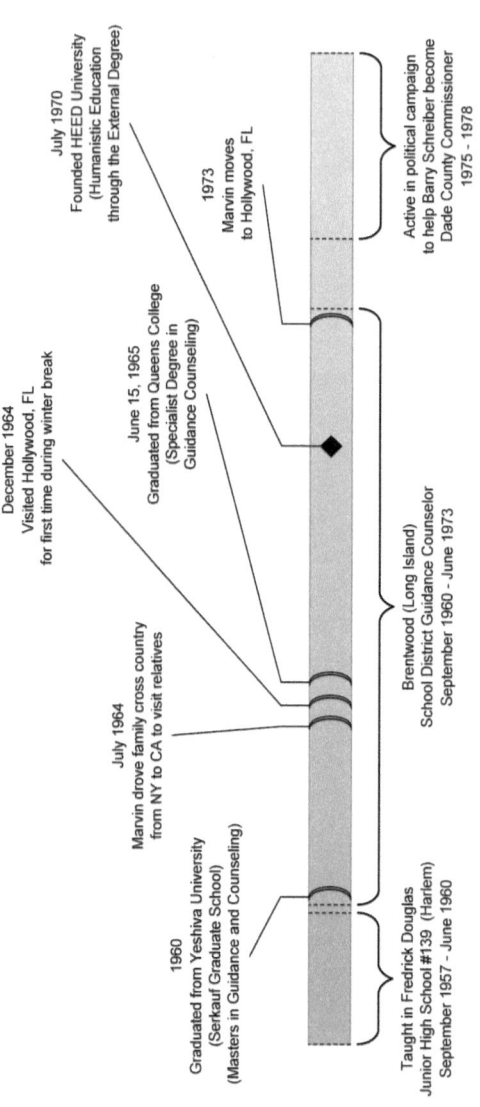

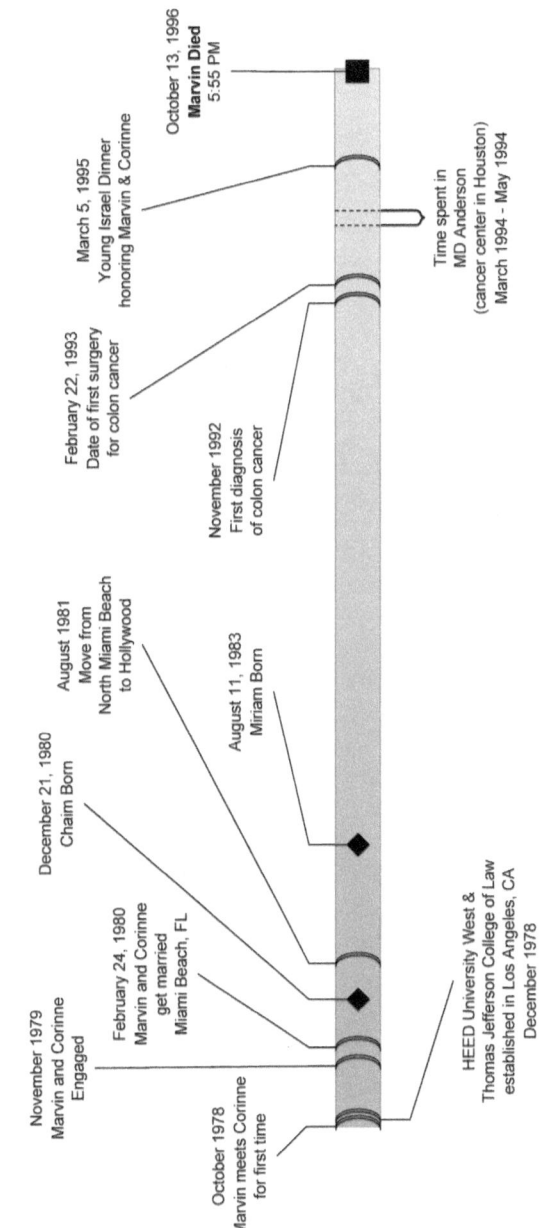

Pictures

Marvin and Irving (1939)

Ida, Irving and Marvin (1941)

Marvin (1941)

Cousin Selma Fenster, Cousin Lawrence Fenster, and Marvin in Linden, New Jersey (1941)

Cousin Gladys Shapoff, Marvin, Cousin Elaine Shapoff and Ronnie in Coney Island (1944)

Marvin and Ronnie (1944)

Marvin at his Bar Mitzvah (March 1948)

Marvin's elementary school diploma
from the Yeshiva of Brooklyn (June 30, 1948)

Marvin graduating from college

Irving, Ronnie, Marvin, and Fradelle
at Pelham Parkway in the Bronx (1950)

Fradelle, Ronnie, Ida, Irving, Grandfather Chaim Fenster,
and Marvin at Ronnie's Bar Mitzvah (October 1955)

Marvin in Brentwood Public Schools,
New York (1958)

Marvin's diploma from Queens College (June 15, 1965)

Remembering Marvin

Irving, Fradelle, Ida, Marvin, and Ronnie at graduation party in honor of Fradelle's graduation from Hunter College (June 1971)

Miriam Friedman (secretary) and Marvin in Brentwood Public Schools, New York

An unknown attorney, Marvin, and Barry Schreiber signing closing documents for HEED University building

Marvin awarding diplomas at HEED University Graduation ceremony with student and Barry Schreiber

Marvin awarding diplomas at HEED University Graduation ceremony

Marvin and Florida Senator Richard Stone

Marvin, Irving, Ida, Ronnie, and Fradelle during Pesach at Sea Gull Hotel in Miami Beach (1976)

Irving, Anna, Ronnie, Ida, Fradelle, and Marvin
at Ronnie and Anna's wedding (November 20, 1977)

Marvin cutting the Challah at Ronnie's wedding (November 20, 1977)

Marvin and Ida

Marvin and Corinne (1979)

Rabbi Leff, Marvin, and Irving at
Marvin and Corinne's wedding (February 24, 1980)

Rabbi Leff and Marvin at Marvin and Corinne's wedding
(February 24, 1980)

Marvin and Corinne on their wedding day
(February 24, 1980)

Marvin and Corinne at Fradelle and Jeff's wedding
(August 19, 1980)

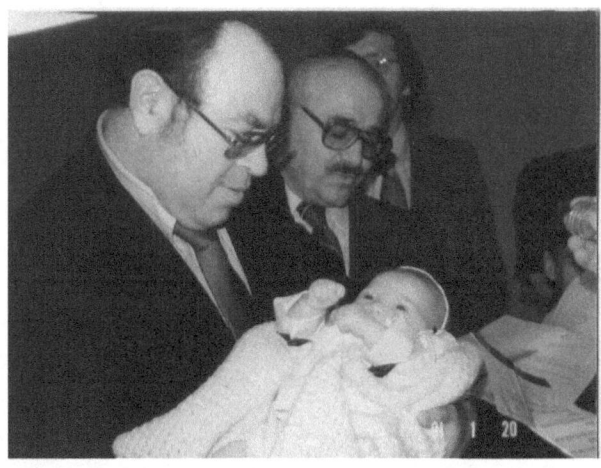

Marvin, Rabbi Vam Schwartz, and Chaim at
Chaim's Pidyon Haben (January 20, 1981)

Marvin and Chaim (December 1983)

Marvin and Chaim (1982)

Marvin and Miriam (1984)

Marvin, Miriam, Ida, and Cousin Irving Shaw (Itznu)
in Hirsch home (1988)

Marvin, Chaim, and Miriam in front of Hirsch home (1990)

Chaim, Corinne, Miriam, Marvin, and niece
Lauren Sall at Niagara Falls (1991)

Bubbie Hennie and Zaidie Paul Sall, Miriam, Corinne, Chaim,
and Marvin in Elmira, New York (1991)

Niece Chaya Hirsch, Miriam, Ida, Marvin, Corinne, Chaim, Anna, Ronnie, Nephew Chaim Milrad, Fradelle Milrad, and Jeff Milrad at Chaim Hirsch Bar Mitzvah (January 8, 1994)

(From Left to Right, Back to Front): Albert Goldman, Selma Goldman, Jerry Heiman, Cousin Gladys Heiman, Karl Bell, Cousin Elaine Bell, David Grossman, Cousin Frances Grossman, Corinne, Marvin, Anna, Ronnie, Fradelle, Jeff, Miriam, Cousin Irving Shaw, Dorothy Winston, Cousin Selma Kotler, Chaim, Ida, Niece Chaya Hirsch, Nephew Chaim Milrad at Chaim Hirsch's Bar Mitzvah (January 8, 1994)

Rabbi Grunblatt, Chaim, and Marvin at Chaim's
Bar Mitzvah (January 8, 1994)

Zaidie Paul Sall, Chaim, and Marvin at Chaim's
Bar Mitzvah (January 8, 1994)

Niece Chaya Hirsch, Chaim, Corinne, Marvin, and Miriam at Chaya Hirsch Bat Mitzvah (1994)

Marvin, Lynette Sookdeo, and Ida at Young Israel dinner honoring Marvin and Corinne (March 5, 1995)

Rabbi Davis and Marvin at Young Israel dinner honoring
Marvin and Corinne (March 5, 1995)

Chaim, Corinne, Marvin, and Miriam at Young Israel Dinner honoring Marvin and Corinne (March 5, 1995)

Epilogue

"Fortunate is he who was raised in the Torah, whose toil was in the Torah, who has given pleasure to his Creator, who grew up with a good name and departed the world with a good name."
(Talmud Berachos 17a)

Epilogue & the Last Day

By Chaim Hirsch

About seventeen years ago, a family faced a difficult decision as to which school their children should attend. The current school was undergoing an administrative makeover and the philosophical direction of the school was unknown. The children were in second and fourth grade, and didn't want to change schools. Their friends weren't switching schools, and they were familiar with their current surroundings. The parents decided it would be best if the children switched to a more religious environment, one that had more emphasis on Jewish education.

The son, entering fifth grade, fussed about how he would miss his friends, teachers, and the short commute. During that summer, the father took the son under his wing and started teaching him new subjects. The father started with something simple, the daily Yom, which is the Psalm unique to each day of the week. He then explained the structure and background of the Gemara (Talmud).

When the new academic year started, the son was fascinated that the things he had been learning over the summer were a hands-on experience in his new setting! The daily Yom was recited (which he had never done before), and the class studied Gemara on the very first day. The end of the first week arrived, and at the Friday night Shabbos dinner table, the excited son decided he would review the entire week's worth of Gemara! Starting on his forty-five-minute lecture, the mother and father realized they had clearly hit a hot button.

The mother and father were my parents, and the son was me. The enthusiasm that I had in learning Gemara and saying the daily Yom wasn't my own enthusiasm. It stemmed from my father having a passion for Torah, which he instilled into me at a young age. As he taught me, when you combine Jewish pride with a Torah lifestyle, your life will be filled with meaning.

The very first verse of the Torah states, "In the beginning, God created the Heavens and the Earth." The Chashava L'Tova gives a novel explanation: "In the beginning (of each day, one should think to themselves that) God created the Heavens and Earth." Meaning that our mundane everyday concerns are devoid of any real meaning if we don't recognize that God is the true Creator. Once we understand it is His will we need to follow, then we can inject meaning into our daily lives.

The Vilna Gaon explains that the word Bereishis is an acronym for the values that fill our lives with meaning:

Letter "Bais" (of Bereishis): This stands for Bitachon (trust) in God

Letter "Reish" (of Bereishis): This stands for Ratzon (desire) to live according to His Will

Letter "Aleph" (of Bereishis): This stands for Ahavah (love) of God, fellow man, and Mitzvos

Letter "Shin" (of Bereishis): This stands for Shtika (silence), refraining from speaking negatively

Letter "Yud" (of Bereishis): This stands for Yirah (reverence) of God, as being complacent can sometimes be negative

Letter "Tav" (of Bereishis): This stands for Torah, for it is only through Torah that one can transform their life into one of sanctity and meaning.

These qualities were the way my father conducted his life. But notice that in order for each of these qualities to work, the one common denominator is the study of Torah – the last letter of Bereishis. Without the Torah, none of them will work. Indeed, my father epitomized his love for a Torah lifestyle, which he clearly wanted to pass on to the next generation.

As a final epilogue to this book, I thought it would be appropriate to outline the final day of my father's life, October 13, 1996, the first day of Rosh Chodesh Mar Chesvan, from my perspective. Of course, because we were in different places at different times, other relatives may have additional, or even slightly different, memories. Here is an inside look of what transpired through my eyes:

Saturday Night: My father had been in the hospital over Shabbos, while the rest of the family was home. Right before Shabbos, he had slipped into a mini-coma, where he wasn't able to talk, but still murmuring and clearly moving. After Shabbos, we immediately went to the hospital, where the doctors told us, as we had already known, his condition was severe. The Rabbeim from Yeshiva Toras Chaim were notified, and Rabbi Grunblatt, Rabbi Palgon, and Rabbi Chait visited that night. They said Tehillim by my father's bed side.

Sunday Morning: When I woke up that morning, I did not know what to do. Should I go to the hospital to be with my father who is, for the most part, unconscious, or should I go to yeshiva for the usual half a day of Sunday school? I eventually decided to go to school, although this would be a question that plagued me for days, weeks, and years afterwards.

8AM – 10AM: At the yeshiva that morning, my Rebbie from tenth grade, Rabbi Flamholtz, was celebrating his son's bris. Obviously there was a lot of simcha and happiness, something that was hard for me to share, knowing the gravity of the situation back at the hospital. During the festive meal of the bris, I recall classmates asking how my father was doing. My limited response conveyed that the situation was not optimistic.

10 AM – 1PM: We had class during this time, but needless to say, it was hard to focus on the material when there were other distractions running through my mind.

1PM – 2PM: School was over for the day, and it was time to go home. I even remember the person who drove carpool, and that there was a Dolphin game that had just begun (although at the time, I was not a big sports fan). The ride home was a quiet one, just thinking about what and if anything had happened back at the hospital.

2PM – 2:30 PM: When I got home, Miriam, my sister, was still there, although my mother was already at the hospital. We quickly ate lunch, and immediately got a ride to the hospital.

2:30 – 5PM: We arrived at the hospital, and just walking into the room revealed the whole story. My father's eyes were closed most of the time, and he faded in-and-out of a quasi-coma. During this time, the entire family surrounded him. His wife, children, siblings, close friends and even my future in-laws. We stood around his bed and watched him, as he continued to fight for his life.

We noticed that my father lifted his hands and made an aimless attempt to throw them in the air. The nurses watched in amazement as he lifted and moved his arms. They glanced over to the monitors and told us that from a medical perspective, his blood pressure was quite low and he should not be able to lift his hands.

While the nurses and others wondered what he was doing and how he had the strength to do it, my mother and I knew exactly what was happening.

Only two weeks earlier, my mother and I were sitting with my father in his bedroom, and my father said, "I know that the Malach Hamaves (Angel of Death) is coming to get me, but I am going to put on my boxing gloves and fight him off." Right there in the bedroom, my father mockingly punched through the air, as his childhood fantasy was to be a boxer.

The punches my father threw in the air as he was dying were no coincidence. He was sending a clear message that he was fighting, no matter how close he was to dying.

5:30 – 6PM: With the entire family around him, we watched as his hand movements got weaker, his breathing slowed, and eventually stopped. We knew that was it, the battle was over at approximately 5:55 PM on October 13, 1996, the first day of Rosh Chodesh Mar Chesvan. The family hugged one another, as a very long struggle had come to an end.

6:30PM – 7PM: My future in-laws drove Miriam and I back to the house, while my mother stayed back to make arrangements with the funeral home.

7PM – 10PM: Back at the house, people poured in to console us. As we were discussing funeral logistics for the next day, I asked about giving a eulogy. I even pulled out from my pocket a few thoughts I had jotted onto a small piece of paper several weeks back. It was at that time that the community Rabbi informed us that it was Rosh Chodesh (beginning of the new month), and in accordance with Jewish tradition, there are no eulogies on Rosh Chodesh.

Then the ultimate twist came. My uncle Ronnie pulled me aside and said that my very humble father had privately requested several days earlier that there not be any eulogies at his funeral. And just like that, he got his wish.

For days, weeks, and even years after that day passed, I questioned my decision to go to yeshiva that Sunday morning. Why did I do it? Was it the right thing to do? If someone had told me at the beginning of the day it was going to be my father's last, would I still have gone?

I may never know the answers to these questions, but one thing I do know for sure: my father would have been proud of the decision, as I was living a lifestyle he and my mother embraced. It was an environment of Torah and ethical values; a place where he prepared me to go so many years earlier. It was a sad day, but one that also paid tribute to my father's life – and served as a vision for how his family would continue living theirs.

Appendix A:

New Stories Received After Original Publication in 2008

United!

By Stuart Dalkoff

In reflecting back 25 years since Marvin is gone, the one thought that came into my mind is that we need more Marvin's now more than ever because he was someone who brought people together and made them feel closer. He drew you near. These days we are all very divided. We need more Marvin's to bring us together and make us feel as if we are united and not apart. Halevai!

Forget the mosquitoes! It's Succos!

By Anne Grabois

As neighbors of the Hirsch's, we were invited to their home one year for Succos. That summer, there was an outbreak of mosquitoes, some of which were possibly carrying diseases. As we entered the Hirsch home for the holiday, there was some concern by the family and friends about eating outside due to mosquito situation. Marvin, however, proudly and emphatically said, "I don't care about the mosquitoes! It's Succos, and it's a Mitzvah to eat in the Succah! I'm going outside to eat in it!" Thankfully, we did not have any mosquito issue, but Marvin's resiliency and passion for performing the Mitzvah was something that has stayed with me to this day.

Everyone is a Person

By Miriam Hirsch

There are, in life, certain memories which will last, certain memories which are cherished, and certain memories which we wish we could remember as if it were yesterday. My father was a man who exemplified many Middos Tovos when it came to Bein Adem l'Chavero. As mention in the past, my father made extra efforts to inquire on other people's well-being. It did not matter if it was a close friend or the delivery man; everyone in my father's eyes was a Tzelm Elokim and therefore mattered to him. This made a big impression in the years of his life when he was sick. He utilized his ability for lending a listening ear to those who helped him in the medical field.

This is a Middah I would like to focus on about my father. I am not going to bring in a specific story but rather use this time to reflect on how this Middah made a difference in other peoples lives to this day. They say that a butterfly can flap it's wings in the ocean and on the other side of the world a hurricane can form. So to, with a simple act of kindness toward others, we can impact the world. A simple smile to a neighbor in the street, a more meaningful "thank you" to the sales women in the store, or just a simple phone call to a lonely friend could make a difference in someone's life.

These are the kinds of acts my father exhibited towards others and towards his family. So many people felt so close to my father because of this. When he would ask someone "how are you," it was not just a generic question. It was a question that ran deep and showed that he cared.

Perhaps this is something we can take away for ourselves, in our own lives, making a difference in small ways that can bring big changes to the world, for the good.

My Big Brother, Continued

By Ron Hirsch

It's absolutely incredulous how time speeds by! Twenty-five years and another Yahrtzeit! At the same time I marvel at how slowly sometimes life seems to pass.

Much has happened over these years. I have no doubt that Marvin is kvelling and shebing nachas from his children, Chaim and Miriam, and their families. He has twelve amazingly wonderful grandchildren; Chaim five and Miriam Haller seven. He has nine fabulous grandnieces and grandnephews that he would love. Fradelle has four grandchildren from Chaim Milrad and I have five from my dear Chaya Lord (yes I said Lord).

We miss him immensely.

May his neshama have an aliya and his memory be for a blessing.

A Special Minyan

By Dr. Leonard J. Hoenig

When Marvin was ill, there were several times that Marvin asked me some medical questions, such as "who was the best doctor for something." As a physician, I usually maintain an emotional distance from patients, so that I can remain objective in my advice. Thus my discussions with Marvin were of a clinical nature.

One exception was when he was too ill to go to shul. I was asked to come to a minyan at his house (which may have been during Succos). I recall that day because it was one of the few times where I felt I had absolute kavanah in davening. Somehow, the objective barrier in the doctor-patient relationship broke down, and I felt the impact of the emotional ordeal that the illness had placed on Marvin. I truly admired his courage in fighting back and seeking out the best possible medical care. I also was uplifted by the effort and importance Marvin placed on davening with a minyan. It really made an impression on me.

Shortly thereafter I decided to attend the daily minyan at shul, first with Shacharis and then with Minchah/Maariv, which I have been doing these past eleven years. In retrospect, I believe one of the reasons I did this was the impression Marvin made upon me that day in his house. Now my son Ezri joins me at the daily minyanim. Marvin had a positive influence on many of us here in Hollywood.

When we moved to Hollywood twenty years ago, we were impressed not so much by the warm climate or beautiful trees. What made our Jewish community so wonderful were people such as Marvin, who was a real mentsch. In many ways, his children are following in his footsteps and inspiring us to achieve greater heights in learning Torah and doing Mitzvos. I am sure Marvin is very proud of the entire family.

Marvin's Only Regret

By Sammy and Sandy Libraty

We got to know both Marvin and Corinne through the association of our children who attended grade school together. Our sons Eli and Michael were in the same grades as Chaim and Miriam, respectively, and frequently got together at each other's houses. To know Marvin and Corinne is to love them.

When Marvin was in the hospital at Hollywood Medical Center, Sammy helped to put Tefillin on Marvin one Sunday morning. When they finished, Marvin insisted that it was time for Sammy to go to work. While Sammy told Marvin that he had carved out time to spend with him, Marvin selflessly persisted that Sammy had other responsibilities and should attend to them. That's who Marvin was – a selfless person who put the interests of others before himself, even when he was sick.

We also found it fascinating how Marvin lamented his only regret. He would say, "I'm only sorry that I won't be able to perform and fulfill Mitzvos once I leave this world." He was truly an exemplary example of a Mitzvos-driven individual whose life revolved around performing the will of Hashem.

In the face of adversity, Marvin taught everyone around him how to behave. While many people let their disease overtake them with depression and negativity (some even ask "why me?"), Marvin was the opposite in his approach and taught others how to behave – and more importantly – live.

While Marvin is greatly missed by his family and friends, we know the impact that he made on people will last for generations.

A Righteous Man

By Fradelle Milrad

Marvin had a way of putting others at ease,
He said and did the little things that would comfort and please.

He had a special kind of warmth and quick to understand,
And whenever there was a need, he'd lend a helping hand.

This world of ours was a better place
And happier by far because of him.

With eternal love and gratitude to you Marvin, Of Blessed Memory, on the 25th anniversary of your passing.

Time went by so quickly but my memories never faded. I miss you and think of you very often and what could have been. You left us too soon but Hashem had other plans.

You would be so proud of Chaim and Samantha and their 5 beautiful kinderlech. And to Miriam and Zev and their 7 beautiful kinderlech. You loved children so much. We taught our grandchildren the tricks you taught your kids and your nieces and nephews. Your name is always mentioned. Our older grandkids read the first book, "Remembering Marvin" and asked so many questions about you wanting to know more about you.

You made a great impact on all those whose lives you touched. You always cared about your family and friends and were always there to lend a helping hand. The world is a better place because of you. Those who knew you had the fortune and pleasure of being in your company.

I know Hashem has you under his wing and is looking after your neshama. You were humble and kind, righteous and loyal, trustworthy and compassionate. You were a virtuous man.

I only wish your grandchildren and your great nieces and nephews knew you. I was privileged to call you my brother. I was so very proud of you.

May we see each other again in eternal and everlasting life. May Moshiach come now. Amen.

Your loving sister,

Fradelle

Even Chasidim Daven at my Minyan!

By Tzvi Schachter

As Marvin got weaker from his illness, it became increasingly difficult for him to walk the full distance to shul. He would rest at about the "halfway" mark between his house and the shul, sitting on a short wall at the corner of 46th Avenue and North Hills Drive. I remember that as he sat there, he would greet everyone with a joyous "Good Shabbos!" as they passed by. He used that resting time to rejuvenate his energy and wish people well.

Towards the end of his life, Marvin was saying Kaddish for his mother who had recently passed. When community members realized he was weak and didn't have the energy to walk to shul, several congregants gathered at the Hirsch home on Shabbos for a minyan, enabling Marvin to say Kaddish for his mother. After the minyan, I remember offering Marvin a "L'Chaim" over some whiskey, to which Marvin jokingly replied, "I have my herring – that's going to be my 'L'Chaim' for now!"

When I would come to davening with my gartel and kapatah, Marvin would joyfully say, "Wow, I must be really special – I even have Chasidim davening at my minyan!" Despite the difficult times he encountered with his mother's passing and his own illness, Marvin maintained his positive, cheerful, and upbeat personality.

Tell Him You're a Kohein!

By Irving Shaw
(Cousin Itzynu, also known as "Itzik De Ballagula")

Most of my encounters with Marvin were during the summers, when I was an instructor at his school, HEED University. One summer, he loaned me an old, brownish color Studebaker, which was donated to the school. I think a summer student gave it to him, and I became the recipient.

One evening, we went out for office supplies and I was driving the car. The car had so many flaws, such as when you tried to use the horn, the glove compartment would spring open! There was a head light out, and as we drove down Sheridan Street, we were stopped by a motorcycle cop.

I knew the cop was Jewish, as I had seen him before, and noticed the Star of David on his bike. Marvin jokingly said I should tell the cop I was a Kohein (Marvin constantly joked that since I was a Kohein, I should receive special honor for my priesthood lineage). Going along with it, I did tell the cop was I was a Kohein, and as a result, the cop gave me a warning ticket! Marvin was bright and generous. When I got stuck on a crossword puzzle, I went to him for help. Imagine him knowing that an aglet was the top of a shoelace!

The World Needs More Marvin Hirsch's

By Irvin Sonnett Stern (AKA: Cousin Sonnett)

This is my remembrance of the multi-talented Professor, Dr. Marvin Hirsch, and his effect on my mother, uncle, and me.

Although I had always heard of the Hirsch family, I had only brief and occasional interactions with them. My earliest recollection of close contact with Marvin was during my work at his school during the summer of the late 1970's. Marvin's school, HEED University, was based on a unique concept at that time. The idea was to allow adults to continue with their careers while studying for an advanced degree.

When I started helping out, I noticed many older, yet intellectually vibrant, adults who were very excited and animated. They had just arrived at HEED University and were getting mentally ready to officially present/defend their thesis reports. Every person was from a different area of the country and each with a different educational emphasis. Everyone knew his or her efforts with HEED University would be of financial and career improvement. Consequently, the experience at HEED University would prove to be an invaluable personal and emotional asset, besides just an intellectual gain.

I also saw how Marvin went out of his way to help family members economically. For some of his family, he made the tuition at HEED University very affordable – so that all could benefit. A person's scholarly ability – not their bank account – was what mattered to him. The family members who specifically benefited from Marvin were his cousins Gladys Heiman, Irving Shaw, and me.

My mother, Gladys Heiman (cousin Gladys Shapoff), was granted a Master's Degree from HEED University. That degree allowed her to get hired by a couple of School Districts in the

California Central Valley (Porterville Schools and the Fresno School District) as a school nurse. That was a major turning point in her life, since she had little financial opportunities elsewhere. Her nursing training/license education from Marvin's University, combined with her K-12 school nursing experience, made her highly in demand. In fact, she is still working as a school nurse to this very day in Southern California.

The other person who benefited from Marvin and HEED University was my uncle Irving S. Shaw, Ph.D. (cousin Itznu). He was a high school teacher for most of his life. While working with special needs pupils (in Arizona and California), he compiled a very extensive and scholarly vision on education theory. In fact, Marvin utilized Irving S. Shaw's dissertation as one of a few examples of the very high competency of HEED's students. That Ph.D. from HEED gave Dr. Shaw a very important emotional and financial boost, in my opinion.

For myself, when I was about to leave Florida to return home in California, Marvin and Ron offered me a wonderful opportunity. I was given a chance to become a California lawyer through their school with very little tuition. Actually, in hindsight, that offer was a gift of a lifetime. Unfortunately, I turned it down and chose a different path for my life.

From stories my mother tells, in the early days of New York, families lived in very close proximity to one another, and that experience created a mental attitude absent today. In essence, it was a heightened world view. I witnessed how Marvin and his family demonstrated that attitude of giving and love for others while I worked for HEED that summer. The world needs more Marvin Hirsch's today.

Visiting Marvin's Grave on My Father's Yahrtzeit

By Rabbi Avrohom Yachnes

There is a widespread custom to visit a deceased parent's kever (grave) on the day of their Yahrzeit. Chazal tell us that if a person is unable to go to the Kever of the parent on the Yahrtzeit, they should instead go to the grave of a Tzadik.

Years ago, on my father's Yahrtzeit, I was unable to go to my father's Kever. I therefore went to visit the gravesite of Marvin Hirsch - a person who I and others in the community admired and considered to be a Tzadik.

Appendix B:

Chaim's Additional Stories, Memories, and Speech Excerpts After Original Publication in 2008

Speech Excerpt from October 17, 2009:

In 1956, a family struggled to pay their bills. The parents worked hard, but didn't have extra money to buy some of the coveted "extras" for their children. The eldest child was fifteen years older than the youngest daughter. The daughter, at the age of six, really wanted to learn how to play the piano. The parents didn't have the money for it, but the older brother, who was twenty-one and realized how important it was to his sister, decided to buy her a piano, telling his parents they could repay him whenever they had the money. The older brother wanted nothing more than to see his youngest sibling happy – even if it meant using his hard earned money on somebody other than himself. I'll clue you in as to who this family was in just a minute.

Now let's jump to 2009. Samantha and I bought a house. The market and timing was right, so we made the plunge. A few weeks after moving in, Samantha reminded me that my mother, who now lives in California but still owns a house in Florida, used to have a piano in the living room. Samantha wondered what ever happened to that piano, and if still available, would be a perfect compliment to our new home.

I called my mother and inquired about the piano. Much to our disappointment, she told us the piano was sold several years ago, and of course, had she known we wanted it, she wouldn't have sold it. Nonetheless, the piano was gone.

On that very same day, I got a striking email from my aunt Fradelle – my father's sister. Unaware about our conversation and interest in my mother's piano, my aunt wrote to me that she wanted to give Samantha and I the piano she had in her house. She proceeded to tell me the significance of the piano and why it carried such sentimental value.

Remember the story I told about the older brother who bought a piano for his little sister? That was my father, who at twenty-one, used some of his first paychecks to buy my aunt this piano. And now, over fifty years later, the piano would find its way into our new house. Until recently, even my own mother never knew the history behind Fradelle's piano.

We graciously accepted the piano from my aunt, as it is now in our new house. When most people look at it, they see a beautiful instrument that has weathered the years well. When I look at it, I see an instrument of chesed and true love. My father used his first hard-earned monies to help his little sister – a clear indication of his chesed and what was important to him. By displaying that unobstructed love to his family, it was a love that would last forever.

Speech Excerpt from October 9, 2010:

Someone from the community recently approached me and shared an unusual episode. They had a dream about my father. The person said the dream started in the house I grew up in (on 49th Avenue), and the person said, "Where am I?" to which my father laughed and responded, "You're in Marvin Hirsch's house, of course!" The individual said that the nature of the conversation flowed, but the one thing they consistently observed was my father's jubilant tone and attitude. He was smiling, laughing, with a positive approach; as if nothing in the world could bother him.

The twist in this story is that the person who had the dream about my father didn't know him. In fact, that person never met him. Of course, they heard many stories I told about him over the years, but they never met him, yet had a dream about him and his positive attitude. Hearing the perspective from someone who did not know him made me appreciate how his general attitude and approach to life was so inspiring.

Another Vignette from October 9, 2010:

  A business colleague of mine recently recommended that I read the book, Tuesdays with Morrie. The book is about a student reuniting with his university professor (Morrie) years later, after learning that his beloved mentor is dying from ALS, Lou Gehrig's disease. The story is about how the student went to Morrie's house every Tuesday and learned about the lessons of life in his final months. Most relevant, I found, was Morrie's incredible perspective and approach to his disease and the way he handled it. He didn't feel sorry for himself and wallow in his own sorrow. He used his disease as an instrument and opportunity for teaching and inspiring others.

  As I was reading the book, I couldn't help but think about the months leading up to my father's death. He died in October 1996, and the summer before that, I finished my freshman year in high school and was unsure what to do that summer. I had worked at a summer camp the year before, but that year, decided it would be best if I stayed home. I had no way of knowing when my father would die, but knew that my time spent with him during that summer would be important for me. During that summer, we spent a lot of time together. We would go to shul, learn Mishnayos and Parsha together, and talk about some of the experimental treatments for cancer he continued to explore.

  After reading the book, Tuesdays with Morrie, I realized I had my own, more subtle version, of the "Summer with Daddy." I was still only a young teenager, and we didn't talk about all the philosophies of life. But it did give me a great insight into who he was and his approach of wanting to do nothing more than live life to the fullest with a Torah mentality. There are no doubts – he worked hard at fighting for his life and even more, maintaining a positive demeanor as best as he could during his declining months.

Vignette from October 13, 2012:

Early in the morning, I was feeding the kids breakfast, and I said to Jake, "Who do I love?" Then I answered to my own question, "I love Rochel, Mommy, Bubbie, Zaidie, Savta…and JAKE!" Then Jake looked at me and said, "Today, my name is not Jake." I laughed and said, "So Jake, what's your name today?" He said confidently, "Today, my name is Mordechai." I was stunned. He had never done that before…and today was the English date of my father's death (October 13).

Birth of Dani on October 29, 2012:

By way of background, some pregnant women have a custom to bite off the pitom of the esrog on Hoshana Rabbah. The significance of this is as follows: According to the Midrash (Bereishit Rabbah 15:7) the forbidden fruit that Chavah ate and also gave to Adam was an esrog. As a punishment, from then on, she and all womanhood would have to suffer pain in childbirth. The esrog is an edible tasty fruit and has a good aroma. The pitom, however, is a hard inedible piece of wood with no aroma. By biting off the pitom, the woman is declaring that she disagrees with Chavah and wants absolutely no pleasure from the etrog. The Gemara (Sotah 12a) says that righteous women of all generations were not affected by Chavah's verdict that womankind should suffer pain in childbirth. Therefore, by disassociating herself from Chavah's iniquity, she prays to Hashem that He grant her a childbirth without pain and complications.

For no reason in particular, Samantha did not bite the pitom off the Esrog during the birth of our first two children. However, as our third baby's due date was around Succos time, it reminded me of that minhag, and then, by extension, the story of the esrog with the Balgley family birth. If you haven't done so already, please read *"Marvin and the Beautiful Dried-Up Esrog" By Rueven and Elka (Robert and Ellen) Balgley* earlier in this book. The story focused on my father's strong feeling that when you use something for a mitzvah, it retains an intrinsic value that brings good mazel.

As a result of these memories and associations, Samantha performed the customary ritual on Succos of biting the pitum off our Esrog. Additionally, when Samantha prepared her "birthing center bag" (e.g., the emergency bag full of clothing, diapers, etc.), we made sure to pack our two esrogim as well (one esrog was mine and one was Barry's).

The morning of October 29, 2012, Samantha woke up in the early morning (around 1 AM) with contractions. She wasn't sure if this was the time the baby was ready to come, so she tossed and turned, eventually calling the birthing center around 3:20 AM to solicit their advice. Even after she got off the phone with them, she wasn't convinced this was the right time. She got back into bed for another few minutes and shortly thereafter said, "Ok, this is it. I'm calling Mom and Dad to come over." She then called Barry and Carole to drive over immediately, so that Barry could stay with Rochel and Jake, while Carole came with Samantha and I to the birthing center.

At exactly 3:39 AM (which I documented on our video camera), we left the house on our way for the birthing center and got there by 4 AM. Shortly after 5 AM, things were a bit slow, so I opened my phone to research the Hebrew date, just to have an idea of which date it might be when the baby is born.

On my phone, I googled a Hebrew-English calendar and found a random web site to convert the date. When I went to the web site, I entered in the English date (October 29, 2012) and submitted it to convert to the Hebrew date. When the conversion came up, it revealed that October 29, 2012 converted to Cheshvan 13, 5773. I was stunned when I saw the advertisement on the right of the screen.

It was one of the "revolving" ads, where the ad refreshes each time a new page is loaded on the web site. There was only one ad on the page, and it said, in large print, "Got Esrog? Your one stop shop for arba minim...." Clearly, it was an advertisement to purchase a lulav and esrog set for Succos. The strange part, however, was that it was already 3 weeks AFTER Succos – this would be the LEAST ideal time to advertise for such products! Clearly it was an outdated advertisement that had not been updated.

I immediately looked over at the open bag that we had brought from home, and indeed, confirmed that we "Got Esrog!" To document this (because I knew nobody would believe me), I whipped out my video camera and silently recorded the image on my phone, showing the web site, date conversion, close-up of the advertisement, and then panned over to the actual esrogim that we had there with us. I thought this was very strange timing, but who knows? Maybe it was a weird coincidence.

The early morning continued, and Baruch Hashem, Samantha gave birth at exactly 9:41 AM (documentation from the birthing center shows it to the exact minute). Minutes after the birth, I started to think how long this process had been. I calculated in my mind the moment when Samantha realized she was in labor. That moment was around 3:30 AM, when she called Barry and Carole to tell them to come over (prior to that, she was feeling labor pains, but wasn't fully convinced it was the time). As my mind started racing, I needed to know the exact minute – not an approximate time – of when that phone call was made. I had a gut feeling about something, but did not tell anyone what I was thinking until I did more investigation.

A few hours later, after the baby was born, I drove home (leaving Samantha with Carole at the birthing center) to help Barry with Rochel and Jake. As I drove home, I called Comcast, our phone provider, and asked them to look up the phone records of the call that morning. I needed to know the exact moment that the call was placed. I gave them my social security number, phone number, and address to verify my account, but they refused. They demanded that I tell them how much my last bill was as final verification of my identify! Of course, I was driving, didn't have access to that info, and didn't know my exact bill off the top of my head. Despite giving them all my other identifying information, they wouldn't tell me. I was so incredibly frustrated, as I was on pins and needles at this point with anticipation of what the answer might be to the exact time the phone call was made.

When I got home, I called Comcast again, and this time, I got our recent credit card bill that had the amount on it. I again asked them to look up the phone records of the call that morning, which they now did! The woman told me her system was showing the phone call was placed at 2:31 AM. She then explained that their system is on central time, so really the call was at 3:31 AM. (I got this documented by going to the Comcast web site, signed into my account, and saw the phone records myself — which I clipped and emailed to myself as proof, because again, I knew nobody would believe me with what I am about to say!).

With that information, I had the final confirmation of what my gut told me a few hours earlier: From the moment Samantha realized she was in labor (at exactly 3:31 AM) until the moment the baby was born (at exactly 9:41 AM), it was **6 hours and 10 minutes.**

And guess what the Gematria of Esrog is? **610!**

To have the 'coincidence' of an Esrog advertisement combined with the duration of the labor equaling the numerical value of the Esrog is startling, especially in light of the history our family has with the Esrog. Just as my father taught the power of a Mitzvah is striking, which led to the amazing esrog story of the Balgley birth, here we are again, years later, witnessing another chapter of his legacy. **Never underestimate the power of a Mitzvah!**

We hope and pray that our new son Daniel Levi will grow up and embrace the values embedded in his name, while also realizing the immense power of every Mitzvah he performs.

Culmination of Mussar Haskel Project in January 2013:

When I was in 8th grade in 1994, Rabbi Palgon – who was finishing his first year at the Yeshiva at that time – invited me to participate in a new project. The idea, in theory, was to have students write the shmuessen delivered by the Yeshiva Toras Chaim (YTC) Rabbeim on a weekly basis and distribute these essays to the local shuls. It was there that the idea of Mussar Haskel was born.

In late 1995, a group of students – myself being one of them – embarked on the project. The first issue was on Parshas Chayei Sarah and we experimented by simply publishing it within the yeshiva first, and then distributing it to shuls in later weeks.

After the first issue was printed, it was clear that these 9th grade students didn't have the writing experience or technical skills to draft a polished publication for the general public on their own merit. Dr. Jacob, through his incredible chesed, graciousness, time, and patience, worked with us to perfect both the thought process and technical writing each week. What resulted in the ensuing weeks was a professional publication – in both content and technical writing. Eventually, the essays were distributed to the local shuls in South Florida and also emailed and faxed to various shuls and yeshivas around the country.

I will never forget my father's elated reaction when I came home on Friday afternoon, erev shabbos, with that very first publication in hand from Parahas Chayei Sarah. He was so enthusiastic and excited that I had been a part of something special – studying, writing, and working with Rabbeim on weekly Torah discourses. He had known about the project for some time, but when he held the publication in his hand, you could see the radiant glow on his face.

You may have expected this reaction (as I did at the time), but I recently came across that very first publication that I so proudly showed him – and I was shocked by what I read. While the content of the shmuess was factual, the writing, organization, and structure were lacking. If I may say so – and hopefully I can because I was the one who primarily wrote it – the product had amateur hallmarks. While keeping perspective – I was only a 9th grader at the time – the quality of my father's reaction was remarkable. This was especially noteworthy considering my father was the founder and president of H.E.E.D. university – a self-study college program – and certainly knew the distinction between a polished product and an amateur effort. Yet he was so enthusiastic and excited to see this publication. I believe there were 2 main reasons for this:

- It wasn't anything great I had done – it was the notion that his son was learning and working on a Torah project – something that he valued dearly throughout his life. His happiness was directly linked to his love for Torah and desire to promote it. When I came home and showed him I was actively involved in disseminating words of Torah, it was an elation that money could not buy.
- My father was the definition of trademark Chesed. He knew how hard I had worked on the first issue, and despite realizing the finished product was anything but polished, he mustered up the enthusiasm and excitement. And I can tell you as the recipient, it meant more to me than you will know.

In the fourth year of the weekly Mussar Haskel publication, the yeshiva published a culmination of all these weekly shmuessen in a book that was sent out as a fundraiser before Rosh Hashanah. The book was named, "Mussar Haskel: Courage to Change." It was a book that truly showed what could be accomplished when students, Rabbeim, and volunteers in the community work together with an altruistic goal in mind.

Now fast forward to 2012. To continue the tradition and in memory of my father's 15th Yahrtzeit (16 years since he died), I worked with the Yeshiva, Hanhala, printers, and graphic designers to create an updated 21st century edition of "Mussar Haskel: Courage to Change" with additional shmussen from former and current Rabbeim.

In January 2013, Samantha and I were honored by Yeshiva Toras Chaim with the Kesser Torah Award that was accepted in memory of Marvin Hirsch. It was there that we announced the launch of the updated edition of Mussar Hashkel.

WATCH THE VIDEO! You can watch the video that paid tribute to my father and explained the launch of the updated Mussar Haskel project. Although it is unlisted on Youtube, you can access it by typing in this link: **https://www.youtube.com/watch?v=QnmYYxbPDzM**

This new sefer became available on Amazon and served as a new fundraiser project for the yeshiva.

Speech Excerpt from October 5, 2013:

Almost 20 years ago, my father had an idea – he wanted to compile a Torah pamphlet on all the reasons why there are big and small letters in the Torah. He wasn't sure of all the explanations himself, but he thought it would be a worthwhile project. He asked if I wanted to work on it, and being that I thought it was an interesting and unique topic myself, I agreed. I was in 8th grade at the time, and I even got an older bachur at the yeshiva to be my chevrusa to help me work on it. I bought a new spiral notebook, and for several weeks, we learned about the various explanations. I documented the reasons, and eventually, like most things in life, got distracted and never finished it.

About 2 years ago, nearly 20 years after my father's idea of documenting the reasons for the big and small letters of the Torah, several events happened in the span of about one week:

    a. At Sedat Shlishit in November 2011, around Chanuka time, Dr. Jaffe casually mentioned that he stumbled across a new sefer, called *"By Divine Design: The Kabbalah of Large, Small, and Missing Letters in the Parshah."* I would soon learn that the publication date was recent, in 2010. I was very surprised to hear this, as it was the first time in almost 20 years that I even heard anyone mention such an idea. After Shabbos, I went home and ordered the Sefer to arrive a few days later.

    b. Over the next few days, I was preparing for a speech I was to give around Chanuka time. I found some interesting topics and started putting them together. When the sefer came in the mail a few days later, I decided to look at that parsha. When I opened it up, I couldn't believe it – the topic and material was practically the same as I had prepared independently!

    c. Just a few days later, I was in Yeshiva Toras Chaim learning as I usually do with Rabbi Palgon, and he brought me something from the past. He asked if I remembered back in 8th grade, he and I discussed several ideas for projects – of course I remembered. He then presented me with a small index card with his (Rabbi Palgon's) handwriting on it. Back from 20 years ago, the index card contained the options of various projects we had discussed. He wrote them all down on this index card. One of them was Mussar Haskel (which, of course, came to fruition), and the other was documenting the reasons for the Big and Small Letters in the Torah. He said he randomly came across the card and said he thought I would like to have it!

The strange part about all of this is that all of these events happened within days of each other! Of course, this could all be a coincidence, or perhaps there is an underlying message to learn. I would suggest that ideas and actions impact future generations. We don't often see it in our lives, but the reality is that what we do makes a difference for us, our children, and the next generation.

Speech Excerpt from Pesach, April 22, 2014:

This Pesach marks the 20th anniversary where I led my first Seder. Not the anniversary of a Seder I have *attended*, but the anniversary of the one I first *led*. Today I am going to share with you the story of how I came to be in charge of that Seder.

In January 1994, I celebrated my Bar Mitzvah. My father had already been diagnosed with cancer a couple years earlier and he had previously undergone surgery to remove colon cancer. Shortly after my Bar Mitzvah, around February 1994, he was scheduled to go to MD Anderson in Houston to have a much more serious surgery to remove cancer from the liver. It was a good plan: go to one of the top cancer hospitals in the country with plenty of time for recovery before Pesach, get plenty of rest, and go into Pesach with fervor. Unfortunately, nothing went accordingly to plan. At the young age of 13 years old, I was about to experience a rollercoaster ride that has stayed with me to this day – and would ultimately culminate into being the leader of my very first seder.

March 18, 1994 was erev Shabbos of Parshas Vayikra. I was spending Shabbos in Miami Beach for one of my classmate's Bar Mitzvah. I never enjoyed being away from home, even for Shabbos – ironically, I guess that never changed with me living here in Hollywood – and it was especially difficult because it was one week before Pesach and my father was still recovering in Houston from the surgery. We were all getting anxious about when he would finally be ready to come home. On that Friday afternoon, erev Shabbos, March 18, 1994, in Miami Beach, I got the phone call. A call from my mother telling me that something unexpected had happened in Houston. My mother explained that while the liver surgery was performed as expected, my father developed an infection shortly afterwards and was hindering his recovery. Over the course of the next few days, his condition had deteriorated significantly, and while my father's brother (Ronnie) was with him during this whole experience, my mother told me she would probably have to go to Houston for Pesach. The plan would be for my Bubbie and Zaidie – who were in Los Angeles for Pesach visiting my other cousins – to immediately leave L.A., come to Florida, and make Pesach for my sister and I. Needless to say, I went into Shabbos stunned, shocked, and demoralized. But more than anything else – lonely and alone.

The week before Pesach arrived, and indeed, my mother travelled to Houston. As my mother had promised, Bubbie and Zaidie cancelled their plans in Los Angeles to be with my sister and I in Florida. They whipped together one of the most miraculous cleaning, shopping, and cooking experiences one has ever seen. My sister and I contributed, but keep in mind we were only 13 and 11 at that time. My Zaidie, who was a very traditional Jew, told me, "Chaim, you're leading the Seder." And that was not something I was prepared to do. But I rose to the occasion. We had other family friends over, maybe 10 people in total, all of whom had the utmost of care and sensitivity to the situation.

As that Pesach unfolded, we received very difficult news about my father's condition – it continued to deteriorate, even after my mother had arrived, and it seemed to only get worse. He was moved to the intensive care unit and my mother spent the Seder in the hospital with my uncle. As the daily updates continued to roll in, I went into the last days of Pesach wondering if my father would ever come home alive. It most certainly did not seem that way. And indeed, I spent this Yizkor, 20 years ago, wondering if he had died over the Chag.

I'm going to leave you with the same exact feeling that I had 20 years ago – with plenty of questions, no closure, and a feeling of uncertainty as to what was going to happen next. I will share the conclusion of this episode in my upcoming Shavuos speech.

But for now, I'm also going to leave you with what got me through that Pesach – it was the knowledge that contrary to my thoughts the week earlier, that I was all alone, I realized that was the furthest thing from the truth. I had my Bubbie and Zaidie who demonstrated an unparalleled love and commitment in what they did. We had family friends coming to do everything they could to help us. And we had a community – right here in Hollywood – that rallied together, doing everything in their capacity to be there for us.

Speech Excerpt from Shavuos, June 4, 2014:

For those of you that were here on the last day of Pesach might remember I spoke about how this past Pesach marked the 20th anniversary from when I led my first Seder. As I explained a few months back, that Pesach was a roller-coaster of a ride for my family. In particular, I mentioned how my father went for liver cancer surgery in Houston the weeks before Pesach in 1994, and how an unexpected infection turned all plans upside down. My mother had to tend to my father and my Bubbie and Zaidie altered their Pesach plans to come and take care of my sister and I here in Florida. I would now like to finish that story from 20 years ago.

In the days and weeks following that Pesach 20 years ago, it was a bumpy road. I received daily updates from Houston on my father's condition. Some days were good, some days begged for improvement. But the cruel reality was that he was in the Intensive Care Unit (ICU) for quite some time, where things looked pretty grim and optimism was low. There was a time that nobody thought he was coming home alive. Miraculously, my father's condition started to improve and sometime in between Pesach and Shavuos, he turned a medical corner. He was removed from ICU and everyone breathed a cautious sigh of relief. My mother returned home to alleviate Bubbie and Zaidie, leaving uncle Ron to tend to my father until they returned. Soon enough, the date was set – my father was set to arrive back home the Friday before Shavuos, May 13, 1994 (that year, Shavuos began on Sunday night, May 15, 1994).

Twenty years ago, Friday afternoon, May 13, 1994 had finally come. I was in school and of course, all day long, all I could think about was what it would be like to see my father again. He was so weak in Houston I hardly spoke to him. What did he look like? What we would talk about? What will we do to celebrate?

The carpool driver pulled into my house early afternoon. I came inside and immediately went into my parent's bedroom with great anticipation. I wondered for so long what it would be like. There were no balloons. There were no cakes. There was no music playing. It was quiet and simple. But miraculously powerful and amazing.

My father was weak and frail, still connected to a portable intravenous. We hugged and sat down, talking about school and some of the most plain and simple of life topics. We even talked about some of the Divrei Torah that I sent to him while in Houston.

But in those few moments, it changed my outlook on life – forever. Suddenly, at the young age of 13, I received a valuable clue as to what was important him – and what is important in life. All the money, houses, and material trappings couldn't buy the happiness I felt. I had just gotten my father back.

Vignette from October 13, 2014:

Without knowing that today was Daddy's English Yahrtzeit, Wally Fingerer called me up for an aliya this morning. David Goldis was the Baal Koreh and after my aliya, David said to me, "I forgot the trup (notes) for the first couple words of the aliya because I was thinking about your father."

Right then, after my aliya, I then told him and Wally that Daddy's English Yahrtzeit date was that day. They couldn't believe it.

Story I Told on October 10, 2015:

In the book, "Remembering Marvin," Rabbi Davis wrote:

> *"When I would visit him, he would insist that I had to tell him a Dvar Torah before I left. No matter what condition he was in, lying in bed or sitting at the table, alert or drugged, he would be floating on a spiritual high when I spoke of Torah. I realized after several of these sessions that his euphoria was not due to my Torah knowledge. Not at all. It was the psychological high that he was able to reach through hearing the words of Torah, no matter if they were brilliant or mediocre. It was not the substance that counted; it was the spirit. To date, I have never been able to reach Marvin's level of spirituality. For me, all of Torah depends upon substance and intellectual ability. Marvin captured something far deeper and meaningful. I always left his presence feeling uplifted."*

On June 22, 2014, I wasn't feeling well, consisting of a headache and fatigue. I was discussing it with Samantha at dinner when

Rochel overheard this and said, "Daddy, can you teach us a new halacha or teach us some other Torah?" I looked at her, as this comment seemed to come out of nowhere, and I said, "Sure...but why are you asking all of a sudden?"

Rochel responded, "because maybe it will make you feel better. You told us a story that when your Daddy wasn't feeling well, he would feel better when he learned Torah."

Rochel was referring to the story that I told them probably 6-9 months ago where my father would not be feeling well and he would ask to learn Torah. Further, he would always say that when he would go to shul and open the Ark to take the Torah out, it was as if he would feel the Kedusha going into his body. He remarked that the time he was in shul was a temporary relief for his pain.

The amazing part of this story is that I told this to Rochel and Jake about six to nine months earlier, and I probably only mentioned it once or twice, but certainly not on a recurring basis. But this is what she remembered. So, I whipped out the parsha book and starting going through the parsha. Jake jumped in, head first as well, and was eager to learn. When we were done, Rochel asked, "Did it make you feel better?"

And as you can probably guess, it certainly did.

Story I Told on October 13, 2015:

Yesterday, at Dunkin Donuts, I ran in to get something quick while Samantha and the kids were in the car. As I was walking in, another elderly man was walking in with his aid. Samantha recognized him – it was Rabbi Malovsky – our elementary school Rabbi who knew my father well! I didn't recognize him at first, but I waited until he ordered and was settled. I then went over and confirmed it was him!

I asked if he remembered Marvin Hirsch and told him that I was his son. He asked about Daddy and then I told him that he had passed 19 years ago and that the Yahrtzeit was later that night. Either way, his eyes lit up – he immediately said to his aid that he received his honorary doctorate from H.E.E.D. University. He was so excited about it. He kept going on and on, telling his aid about Daddy and how he got his degree. He also asked about Ronnie and Fradelle. I gave him brief updates on everyone.

On the eve of Daddy's Yahrtzeit, this was an auspicious meeting! it was almost my father's way of "greeting everyone with a happy face." Amazing that he is able to make someone feel special even when he is no longer here.

Email from David Goldis on October 7, 2016:

"I got tears in my eyes this morning, as I turned on the lights by your Dad's plaque in the Shul. 20 years already, on Lamed Tishrei. I remember as if yesterday, being with him that morning...And I could never forget the twice daily visits to the house/ hospital, in the morning to help him with tefillin, and in the afternoon, to schmooze with my buddy. I miss being with him in Shul every day, he was truly one of the good guys, and I'm lucky to have had him as a friend."

Speech Excerpt from October 29, 2016:

On June 8, 2015, I got Gelila in shul and I came home and had breakfast with the kids. I told them that I was so excited that I got Gelila and that there was someone who used to always tell me that Gelila was one of the highest and most important honors you can get. I asked "Do you know who used to say that?"

Jake answers, "Your Daddy." I was shocked, because (a) I don't remember ever telling him that and (b) it was NOT around the yahrtzeit and I wasn't talking about my father at all. I found it especially interesting that Jake associated "special things" (e.g., my excitement about Gelila) with "special people" (e.g., my relationship with my father.)

Speech Excerpt from October 21, 2017:

A year ago, on November 1, 2016, it was the first day of Rosh Chodesh Mar Cheshvan – exactly 20 years on the Hebrew calendar from when my father passed. A very unusual and amazing story happened in the Young Israel of Hollywood-Ft. Lauderdale that day. I attended the 6 AM minyan as I unusually do during the weekday and due to the fact that I sometimes have to leave early, I sit in the back left-hand side of the Shul instead of my normal seat, which is closer to the front right-hand side. As the Baal Korei started reading the Torah for Rosh Chodesh, the Gabbai called a person up to the Torah, and as the name was called, I had several observations that, when combined, sent chills down my spine:

1. *NAME:* My Father's Name was Prominently Pronounced: The Gabbai, Paul Ginsberg, said, "Yamod Moredechai Ben Yitzchak…" and then he fumbled with the final name. As he struggled to find the exact name in his little book, he then said the final name and repeated the whole name: Mordechai Ben Yitzchak Natan. Of course, my ears perked up because the Gabbai "just happened" to fumble on the final name, so he very clearly pronounced my father's name – which was Mordechai ben Yitzchak – in the process of calling up the individual! Immediately after davening, I went over to Dr. Ginsberg and confirmed that the manner in which I heard the events unfold were accurate.

2. *PLACE*: As I started davening mussaf, I got chills down my spine when something else occurred to me. The individual called up to the Torah was Dr. Mark Lamet (interestingly enough, whose son Ari is a former classmate of mine from high school). Dr. Lamet sits in the <u>exact same seat</u> that my father used to sit in. He sits directly next to Al Cohen and at times one seat over from him, which are the two seats that my father and I sat in when I was growing up. Although sometimes there are visitors or newcomers who sit in that area, to the best of my knowledge and observation over the last number of years, there has never been another person in the history of the Young Israel to have ever sat in those seats in the consistent manner that my father and I did – other than Dr. Lamet!

3. *DATE*: This all happened on my father's Yahrtzeit – exactly 20 years after he passed. I've been in the Young Israel plenty of times alongside Dr. Lamet. In general, I am at the Young Israel 6 days a week and have been going for over 30 years. I've never heard any names similar to my father ever called out. But strangely enough, this all happened on the day of the yahrtzeit, exactly 20 years later.

It was as if Hashem was saying that my father's neshama and presence is still here!

Speech Excerpt from October 2018:

I was only 16 when my father died, but in those last couple years, I learned valuable lessons that I will never forget. For example, I would remember having a seder and learning

Mishnayos with my father. We did Rosh Hahsnah, Yoma, and Succah. Towards the end of his life, he was very weak and had little energy to learn. But he would say, "Chaim, the learning of the Torah makes me feel better." As I documented on page 32 of "Remembering Marvin":

> *"My father always had a passion for learning Torah. Whenever I had a day off from school or was on vacation, he would motivate me to learn with him. Over the course of several years, we finished the Mishnayos of Rosh Hashanah, Yoma, and Succah, among other random works along the way. I expected, as he got sicker with time, that his physical desire to learn would diminish, and it would be with less intensity. But I was wrong. In fact, it was just the opposite. Towards the end of his life, when he was sleeping almost two-thirds of the day, he would wake up, and tell me to bring over a Chumash or Mishnah to learn. Even if it was small in time, it was very big in energy and enthusiasm.* **And incredibly enough, after we would learn each time, he would say, "I think I feel a little better."** *His desire to learn never diminished or vanished. Instead, it was actually fueled by his illness, and while most people would have lost interest, he wanted to use every remaining moment to the utmost of its potential."*

This past February 2018, I had an interesting experience that brought back these memories from 21 years earlier. I went to go learn with one of my Rabbeim who I have maintained a relationship with all of these years since high school, Rabbi Mordechai Palgon. When I walked in his house to learn with him, he was laying on his couch horizontal. He was in excruciating neck and back pain. I offered to go home but he wanted to learn. We talked on a variety of hashkafa issues, including how stress can impact a person. I also shared with him

a Rashi that I had prepared. He enjoyed the observations we had on it. However, at the very end of when we were about to leave, he said that when I had gotten there originally, he was in pain, but compared to after the learning session, he now felt much better. It was very inspiring for me to hear that for two reasons:
1. That that was almost the exact same thing that my father told me 21 years ago when he was sick. And I had not heard anyone else say that since.
2. The Gemara (Sanhedrin 19b) says that one who teaches Torah to his friend's child is considered as if he fathered him. So the only two people I have ever heard that from are my biological father and my Rebbie whom I have a close kesher and learn Torah!

Story that Occurred on October 9, 2018:

On the night of October 8, 2018, it was my father's Yahrtzeit. I decided to learn the Zera Shimshon in both Hebrew and English. I opened the English (volume 1) and then subsequently went through it in the Hebrew version as well. I noticed that the Hebew version extended the commentary with many more paragraphs beyond the English version and there were 10 more paragraphs.

In honor of my father's yahrtzeit, I pushed myself to learn the next 2 Hebrew paragraphs (there was no English for it), and I was pretty sure I understood it properly, but I was hoping to ask someone about it later in the week to make sure I translated it accurately. I was unable to go any further, but at least I had done those two paragraphs.

The VERY next day, someone forwarded me a link to the new Artscroll Zera Shimshon Volume 2, with a free excerpt. I decided to open the link and quickly look at it. The very first page in the free download was the English translation of the

<u>exact</u> two paragraphs I had learned the night before and needed clarity on! And there it was, right in front of me!

It's important to note that (1) These were the <u>only</u> two paragraphs translated out of the ten! (2) It was the <u>very first</u> page that pulled up on the download! (3) It was literally the <u>morning after I learned it</u>, where I was wondering if I understood it properly!

Hashem gives you exactly what you need when you need it! And to think this was all on my father's Yahrtzeit!

Story that Occurred on October 11, 2018:

Samantha was settling into her new office at Mizrahi Torah Academy on the JCC's campus in Plantation. For several weeks, Samantha has not been getting any mail at the school. It was a long drawn out process where she spoke to the front office at the JCC and they told her that she would need to contact the post office and let them know that she was in the building in the back with a different address. Without notifying them, they would have no idea that she was there. So for several weeks, no mail was being delivered to her directly.

On October 10, 2018, she called the post office in the morning and was on hold for, with no exaggeration, over 3 and a half hours. When she finally got through to somebody, they told her that she needed to speak with three different departments to answer her questions. While this was incredibly infuriating and frustrating, she ventured out to call those departments.

A little while later, out of nowhere and for the first time in the six weeks that school has been in session, the mailman just walked into her office while she was still on hold with the post office! Her mouth dropped open and couldn't believe it! She told him that she was on the phone with the post office, to which he said, "They'll never pick up the phone, tell me what I can do for you!" Samantha told him her issues, including inquiring where she should hang the mailbox. He was able to answer all the questions and told her that he would make sure that everybody knew that she was on the route.

She asked how he knew to come in and he said the front desk at the JCC told him where MTA was located! It was wild that after six weeks of not showing up at all – and then Samantha being on the phone for multiple hours – the mailman walked in to answer her exact questions.

To make matters more interesting, she asked him his name, to which he replied, "Marvin." It was interesting to note that yesterday was my father's Hebrew yahrtzeit and today was the commemoration of the funeral 22 years earlier!

Story that Occurred on February 27, 2019:

I was travelling to Boston for one night on work and I got together with Jack and the Mike Bailen – our former neighbors from 49th Avenue. Our arranged timing was perfect. I arrived at my hotel and they were literally there to pick me up less than five minutes later! We went to a kosher restaurant in Brookline and had a great time. They asked about everybody in the family and we reminisced about all of the old times in Florida.

Jack mentioned two vignettes about my father that I thought were interesting. First, he mentioned that when my father would see Jack on Friday afternoon, he would holler into the kitchen where my mother was and ask if Jack and Ann could come for Friday night dinner. He remembered this happening quite often and how my mother was so receptive and having them over.

Second, he remembered how my father would call him up out of the blue to have coffee. It meant so much to Jack that my father formed that relationship and constantly was interested in how he was doing. It was fascinating to see what people remember over 20 years later!

Story that Occurred on December 29, 2020:

    I was talking with Dr. David Tepper, who shared with me that in the final days of my father's life, he would bring his son Dov, who was only a child at that time, to meet my father for a very specific reason. Dr. Tepper told his son that he would rarely have an opportunity to meet somebody who is a simple "Pashut Yid" who was also a Tzadik. Dr. Tepper explained that to meet a person with my father's character traits was a rare commodity and he wanted his son to meet him because there are not many people like that.

Story that Occurred on January 14, 2021:

    For the full appreciation of this story, please see the story that I told during a speech on October 21, 2017 (but the story actually occurred on November 1, 2016) as an introduction to this vignette.
    On my 40th birthday, December 21, 2020, my mother wanted me to go for a colonoscopy, since my father had colon cancer at age 55. I was hesitant to go, and even the doctors informally and initially said I could wait until 45. But I decided that to honor my mother, I would go for an official consult.
    I went to Dr. Mark Lamet in late December 2020, and after talking it through with him and noting that I had other stomach-related issues at times, he agreed that I should have a colonoscopy performed. It was scheduled for January 14, 2021, and his son, Ari Lamet (who was my classmate in high school!) performed the actual procedure.
    It's a good thing I did it, because they found six polyps. Three were small, two were large, and one was very large. They

sent it for biopsy, and Baruch Hashem, they were not cancerous. I asked both Dr. Mark and Ari Lamet what would have happened if I waited until I was 45 to get a colonoscopy, and they didn't want to even think about what would have happened.

It wasn't until March 2021 when Dr. Lamet was davening next to me in shul during the week that the whole picture came together for me through three amazing facts:
1. The only reason I went for the colonoscopy was to honor my mother – because of her concern of the heredity risk.
2. We know the Torah's reward for honoring your parents is long life.
3. Then, the doctor who I consulted with – and who agreed I should have a colonoscopy performed – was none other than the person who (a) has my father's same Hebrew name and (b) sits in the same seat as my father did at Young Israel (which I all learned about on my father's 20th Yahrtzeit! See the excerpt from the speech on October 21, 2017 above for full details).

You can draw your own conclusions how this sent chills down my spine when I realized all of these facts combined!"

Story that Occurred on January 24, 2021:

Last night, Rabbi Bentzion Chait gave a Mussar Vaad online. At the end of his speech, he told the story about when my father was with Ronnie in Houston and specifically, the incident with the Malach Hamaves (angel of death). The essence of the story was that my father saw the angel of death approaching, asked Ronnie to immediately say Tehillim, and then the angel of death started to back away. You can read the full details in an earlier chapter of this book, under the title, *"The Angel of Death & the Power of Tehillim."*

Although I did not hear it myself, my understanding is that Rabbi Chait mentioned my father by name and when the person listening heard this, they immediately started recording it in order to send to me. It was amazing to me that Rabbi Chait remembered the story nearly 25 years later!

Story that Occurred on May 12, 2021:

I went to learn with Rabbi Palgon at Yeshiva Toras Chaim for our weekly learning session. We were in the Bais Midrash finishing our session when suddenly, Maariv started. We didn't want to disturb anybody davening while we continued learning, so we walked out into the hallway to continue our learning.

As we were in the hallway and I was explaining a Dvar Torah to Rabbi Palgon, he suddenly pointed to a plaque on the wall next to where we were standing and smiled. I looked over and noticed it was a memorial plaque in memory of my father. I looked in disbelief because I was unaware that that it even existed! Rabbi Palgon said he was unaware of it as well!

When I asked him how he knew it was there, he said he didn't! He thought it was amazing (as did I) that right in the middle of my Dvar Torah, his eyes fixated on the plaque! Had we not been interrupted by Maariv in the Bais Medrash, we never would have been walking in the hallway to see the plaque!

www.ingramcontent.com/pod-product-compliance
Lightning Source LLC
Chambersburg PA
CBHW031242290426
44109CB00012B/408